From the Restaurants of
VAIL
A Mountain Town's **Cookbook**

Enjoy a Taste of **VAIL**
in **Your Own Kitchen**

Park City Publishing / Park City, Utah 2019

Dedication

Dedicated to Cameron and Ashley.

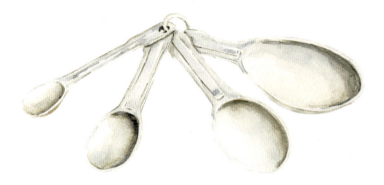

Published by Park City Publishing / Lauren Nadler Designs.
Copyright © 2019 Lauren Nadler and Park City Publishing.
All rights reserved under International and Pan-American Copyright Conventions.
Published in the United States by Park City Publishing and Lauren Nadler Designs, Park City, Utah.
Recipes copyright © accredited restaurants.

Cover and Book, Concept and Design by Lauren Nadler

ISBN: 978-0-9975910-5-7

1 2 3 4 5 6 7 8 9

All images in this book have been reproduced with the knowledge and prior consent of the
individuals concerned. Every effort has been made to ensure that credits accurately comply with information supplied.

Printed in China.

Letter from the Publisher

It took four trips to Vail and much help to find the restaurants that are featured in this book – but 'oh boy' was it worth it! We have met some amazing chefs and owners and drooled over their recipes, cooking our favorites each night as production progressed. We've included wonderful restaurants from areas close to Vail Village including Beaver Creek, Edwards and Avon.

These recipes whave been contributed by chefs of 14 different restaurants, written in their own words. We have strived to make the recipes as consistent, clear, and 'home cook' friendly as possible.

Special note: Several of the restaurants describe, in their recipes, the use of plastic wrap in the oven. Of course the immediate question is "How?" The answer is that restaurants use professional grade plastic wrap which has a different chemical composition to that of typical retail wraps.

The temperatures given for the recipes are in Fahrenheit.
For photograph locations see photo credits page 168.

—*Lauren Nadler*, PUBLISHER, CREATIVE DIRECTOR

Acknowledgments

A huge thank you to all the restaurants and chefs who have contributed their recipes and stories to these pages and endured my repeated visits and phone calls to collect all the information necessary to put this book together.

A special thank you to my husband, Roger, for taking the time, over and over again, reading through the pages of this book. I think that I can now turn over our household cooking to him as he is now an expert chef. We also need to thank my son, Cameron Nadler, a sommelier currently working as Beverage Manager at The Ralph Lauren Polo Bar, one of New York City's top restaurants. Cameron researched many of the wine pairings for the restaurants from their wine lists and, when not available, from his own experience and knowledge of wines. For several restaurants he stepped in to give descriptions of wines that were chosen by the restaurant's Sommeliers.

Further thanks to those who have helped along the way: Michele Martens for contacting the chefs and restaurant owners to bring them on board. Stephanie Edelman, my spelling guru, for taking the time to do a read through. Sheila Jackson for joining us during the final stages of production to work as a copy editor. And to Pat Cone for his photo trips to Vail working with some of the restaurants to help showcase their wonderful dishes and for his amazing images of Vail's beautiful scenery.

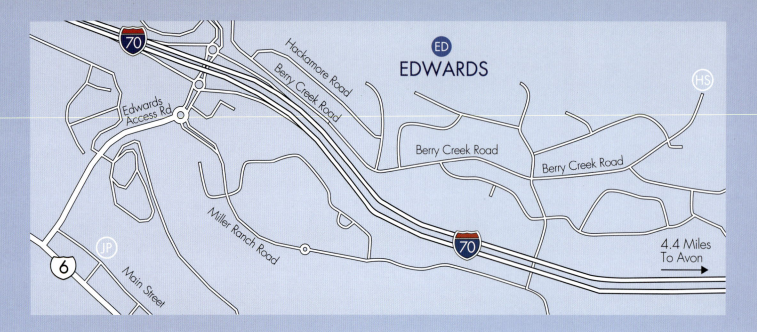

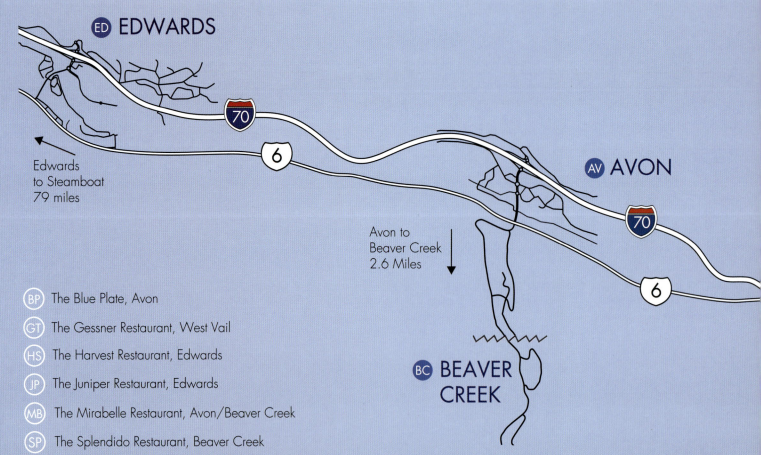

- (BP) The Blue Plate, Avon
- (GT) The Gessner Restaurant, West Vail
- (HS) The Harvest Restaurant, Edwards
- (JP) The Juniper Restaurant, Edwards
- (MB) The Mirabelle Restaurant, Avon/Beaver Creek
- (SP) The Splendido Restaurant, Beaver Creek

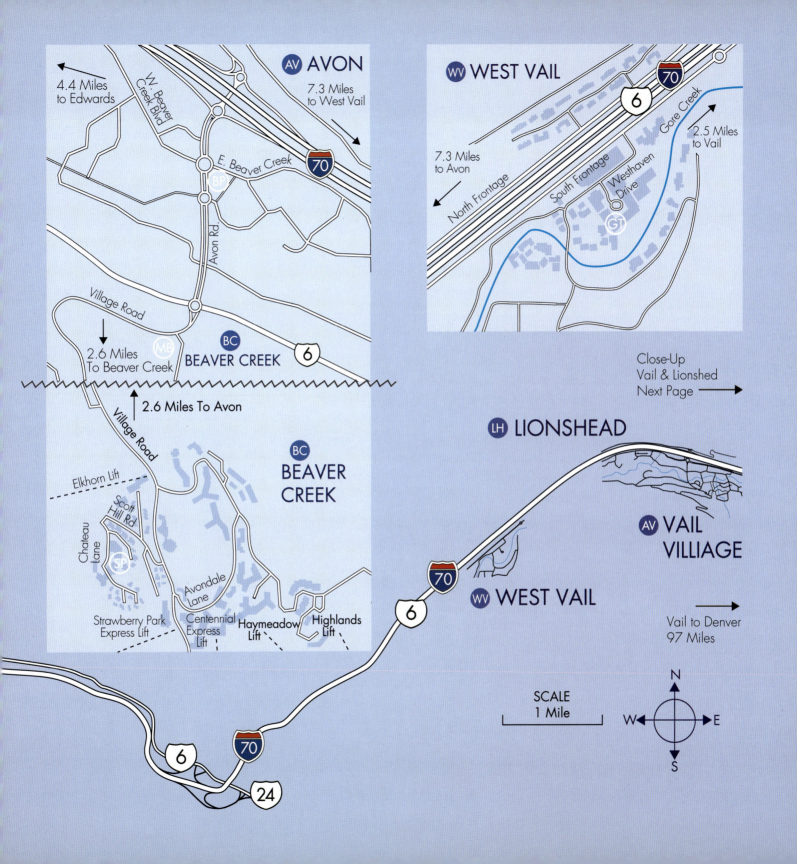

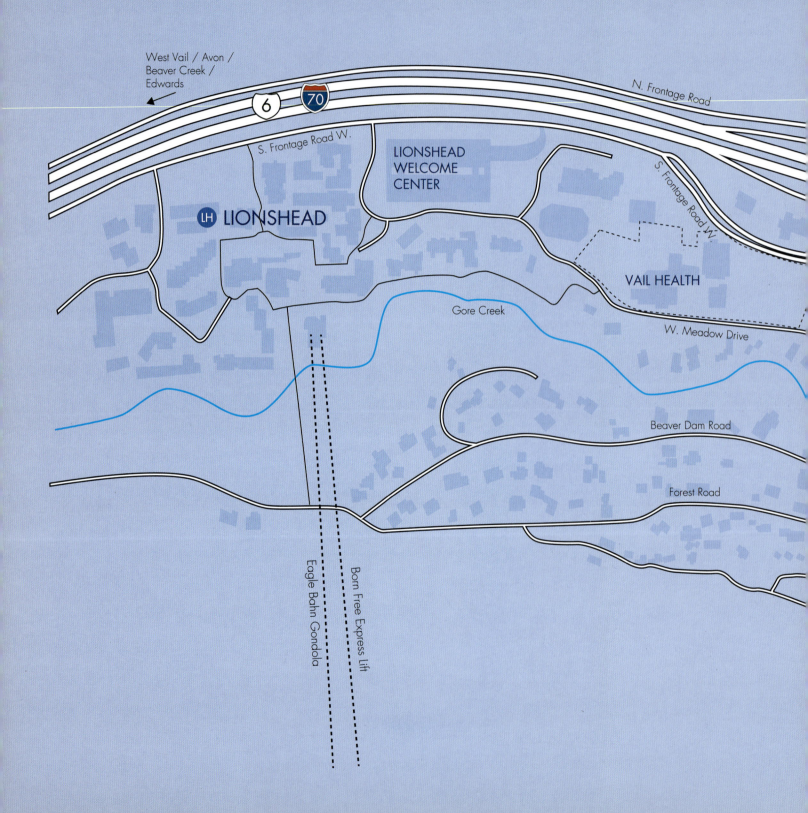

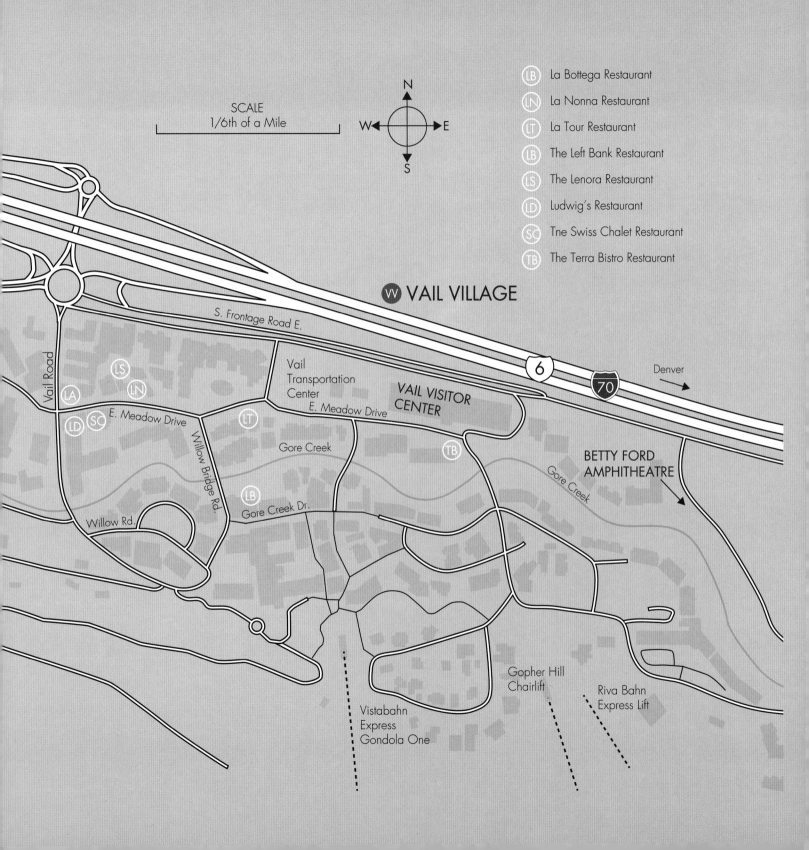

CONTENTS
and Key Code

AV Avon   BC Beaver Creek   ED Edwards   LH Lionshead   VV Vail Villiage   WV West Vail

A Appetizer   S Soup Salad   E Entrée   SD Side Dish   D Dessert

AV BLUE PLATE		**1**
APPETIZER	Harak Isbaao	4
APPETIZER	Vietnamese Meatballs	5
ENTRÉE	Lamb Shank "Shakria" with Yogurt Sauce	6
ENTRÉE	Feather Ribs with Pickled Jalapenos	7
DESSERT	Palisade Peach Marmalade	8
WV GESSNER AT HOTEL TALISIA		**13**
APPETIZER	Smoked Trout Deviled Eggs	16
SOUP	Butternut Squash Soup	17
SALAD	Watercress Salad with Blue Water Dressing and Black Garlic Aioli	18
ENTRÉE	Braised Colorado Lamb Shank, Brussel Sprouts, Lemon Miso Carrots, Parsnip Puree, and Golden Raisin Gastrique	19
SIDE DISH	Ratatouille	21
DESSERT	Coconut Flan	22
ED HARVEST		**25**
APPETIZER	Shrimp Bruschetta	28
SOUP	Gazpacho	29
ENTRÉE	Steamed Mussels with Nduja and Parsley in Saffron broth	30
SIDE DISH	Colorado Lamb Shank with Hand Rolled Potato Gnocchi, Roasted Pumpkin, Green Beans and Sage Brown Butter	31
DESSERT	Strawberry-Rhubarb Cobbler	33
ED JUNIPER		**37**
APPETIZER	Grilled Mediterranean Octopus with Grilled Eggplant, Watercress, Frisee and Romesco Sauce	40
ENTRÉE	Potato wrapped Alaskan Halibut with Rock Shrimp-Corn Succotash, Pickled Red Onion & Herb Oil	41
ENTRÉE	Veal Scaloppini with Angel Hair 'Caprese', Asparagus, Lemon Beurre Fondue and Veal Reduction	42
SIDE DISH	House Made Butternut Squash Raviolis with Toasted Hazelnuts and Pomegranate Molasses	43
DESSERT	The ORIGINAL Sticky Toffee Pudding Cake	44
VV LA BOTTEGA		**47**
APPETIZER	Bruschetta with Duck Foie Gras and Palisade Peaches	50
SALAD	Tenderloin of Beef Carpaccio with Parmigiano Reggiano, Organic Arugula and Truffle Cream	51
ENTRÉE	La Ribollita, White Tuscan Bean and Vegetable Soup	52
SIDE DISH	Fettuccine with Jumbo Wild Prawns "Fra Diavolo"	53
DESSERT	Strawberries with Marsala Zabaglione	54
VV LA NONNA		**57**
APPETIZER	Polpo	60
ENTRÉE	Gemelli alla vodka	61
ENTRÉE	Lamb Chops Agnello Ai Fichi	62
SIDE DISH	Polenta and Broccolini	63
DESSERT	Torta di Ricotta	64

Contents con't

LA TOUR — 67
- APPETIZER — Steak Tartare, Baby Arugula, Quail Eggs and Sauce Ravigote — 70
- SOUP — Truffled French Onion Soup with Braised Short Rib — 71
- SALAD — Field Green Salad with Toasted Goat CheeseDried Cranberry, Pine Nuts, and Whole Grain Mustard Vinaigrette — 72
- ENTRÉE — Dover Sole Meunière with Haricots Vert, Baby Creamer Potatoes with Lemon Brown Butter Sauce — 73
- DESSERT — Crème Brûlée Flambé with Grand Marnier Macerated Berries — 74

LEFT BANK — 79
- APPETIZER — Waygu Tartar — 82
- APPETIZER — Lobster Roll — 83
- ENTRÉE — Fresh Alaskan Halibut — 84
- ENTRÉE — Elk Chop and Red Wine Sauce with Wild Mushrooms — 85
- DESSERT — Chocolate Mousse Cake — 86

LENORA AT THE SEBASTIAN — 91
- APPETIZER — Ono Crudo with Crunchy Garlic and Yuzu — 94
- APPETIZER — Elk Tartare with Hazelnut and Blueberries — 95
- ENTRÉE — Crispy Octopus with Fingerling Potatoes and Chorizo — 96
- SIDE DISH — Cornmeal & Buttermilk Fried Chicken with Honey and Lemon — 97
- DESSERT — The Sebastian Strawberry Snowball — 98

LUDWIGS AT SONNENALP — 103
- APPETIZER — Bavarian Eggs Benedict — 6
- APPETIZER — Sonnenalp Ham & Cheese Quiche — 7
- ENTRÉE — Ludwig's Waffles — 8
- SIDE DISH — Sonnenalp Chocolate Croissants — 9
- SIDE DISH — Sonnenalp Acai Bowl with Homemade Granola — 11

MIRABELLE AT BEAVER CREEK — 115
- APPETIZER — Seared Jumbo Scallop Colorado Summer Corn Alysa Purée with Prosciutto Dust — 118
- SALAD — Ravioli with Carrot Honey Lavender, Confit of Duck, Colorado Goat Cheese Cream and Brussels Sprout Leave Salad — 119
- ENTRÉE — Organic Free-Range Chicken Breast (sous vide) in Olive Oil, with Apple Gratin Potatoes — 120
- SIDE DISH — Colorado Peach Cream Cheese Cake — 121
- DESSERT — Mirabelle Cookie Assortment — 122

SPLENDIDO AT THE CHATEAUX — 127
- APPETIZER — Elk Carpaccio — 130
- SOUP — Porcini Soup — 131
- ENTRÉE — Colorado Rack of Lamb — 132
- SIDE DISH — Crab Fettuccini — 133
- DESSERT — Lemon Custard, Sorbet, Fennel Crumble, Olive Oil Gel — 134

SWISS CHALET AT SONNENALP — 139
- APPETIZER — Käse Fondue — 142
- ENTRÉE — Züricher Geschnetzeltes — 143
- ENTRÉE — Potato Rösti — 144
- SIDE DISH — Käsespätzle — 145
- DESSERT — Apfelstrudel (Apple Strudel) — 146

TERRA BISTRO — 149
- APPETIZER — Baked Ricotta with Tomato Jam, Fennel Sausage, and Garlic Toast — 152
- SOUP — Turmeric and Coconut Cauliflower Soup — 153
- ENTRÉE — Seared Scottish Salmon with Green Goddess Hummus and Zhoug — 154
- SIDE DISH — Tres Leches Shortcake with Caramel-Rum Sauce and Sweetened Whipped Cream — 155
- COCKTAIL — Kombucharita — 156

Restaurant Listing 161
Measurement Guide 162
Sommelier Bio 164

Watercolor Illustrator Bio 164
Photographer Bios 166
Photo and Illustration Credits 166

ENJOY!
From the Restaurants of

VAIL

Blue Plate

BLUE PLATE
AV

CHEF ADAM ROUSTOM

The Blue Plate in Avon, Colorado, is the home and heart of Chef Adam and Elli Roustom. It is a place to gather and simply share a good meal with good people. Top-notch food and drinks without the fuss. As Elli likes to say, "Bring your kids and your hairy uncle alike. We cater to all."

The cuisine is a "melting pot." Chef Adam takes inspiration from here, there, and everywhere. He likes to call it Americana cuisine. At Blue Plate, you can travel to Asia via the tangy tempura fried shrimp or to the Mediterranean with the creamy Damascus hummus. Next, you may voyage to Europe with the melt-in-your-mouth Austrian schnitzel or return to America for the perfectly fried New England-style fish n' chips. And don't forget to try the Leaning Tower of Blue Plate meatloaf, which blends classic flavors from America, France, and Syria (oh my!). As Chef says, "We like to have fun with our food."

Of course, what's a great meal without a nicely paired beverage? Blue Plate has a constantly-rotating selection of fine wines and beer from around the globe, as well as an ever-changing and ever-tasty menu of signature cocktails. Whether you have an idea of what you're looking for in a wine or you're a complete novice, Elli is the woman to talk to. She prides herself in the variety and excellence of her selection, and she likes to keep her prices reasonable.

So, come one, come all. Don't worry about changing your shirt or putting on slacks (however, please DO wear bottoms of some sort!). Simply collect the crew and come savor Blue Plate's fantastic food with the people you enjoy.

Chef Adam Roustom first experienced the grit and grind of working in a restaurant kitchen during the summer of '84 while slinging subs and Greek pizzas for the Kalkanis family in Wareham, Massachusetts.

Yet, his passion for cooking as an art form did not truly develop until 15 years later, as he pursued his second degree at the New England Culinary Institute.

Since he's worked with such distinguished chefs as Lydia Shire of BIBA and Bernard Guillas of The Marine Room at the La Jolla Beach & Tennis Club. He always knew he wanted to start his own restaurant.

When he opened the Blue Plate in 2009, he wanted to create a place where he himself would enjoy eating, and where his patrons could "eat fine dining quality food without all the fuss and knife cuts."

Blue Plate
Harak Isbaao

LENTIL & PASTA
1 cup lentils
½ cup vermicelli pasta, cut into 1 inch strips
4½ cup water
½ tsp kosher salt
2 Tbsp tamarind
2 Tbsp pomegranate molasses
½ tsp bharat seasoning
½ tsp kosher salt

POMEGRANATE MOLASSES
4 cups pure pomegranate juice
⅔ cup sugar
⅓ cup freshly squeezed lemon juice

BHARAT
½ cup ground cinnamon
½ cup ground nutmeg
¼ cup ground all spice
¼ cup black peppercorn
2 Tbsp dry galangal
1 Tbsp ground clove

CRISPY ONIONS
1½ cup canola oil
1 yellow onion, Frenched

GARLIC & CILANTRO
8 cloves garlic
1 bunch cilantro
6 Tbsp extra virgin olive oil

FRIED PITA
2-3 loaves pita bread
1½ cup canola oil

GARNISH
pomegranate seeds

Lentil & Pasta
Put lentils, salt and water into a pot and bring to a boil. Once lentils are tender, add pasta and cover until pasta is cooked through. Once tender, add the tamarind, pomegranate molasses, bharat seasoning. Add salt, if necessary.

Pomegranate Molasses
A store bought pomegranate molasses is suggested. To make your own follow this, Blue Plate approved, version. Pour the pomegranate juice, sugar, and lemon juice into a small saucepan. Bring to a light simmer over medium heat. Stir to dissolve sugar. Reduce heat, continue to stir to dissolve sugar, and simmer very lightly for 60-80 minutes. Stir every 10 minutes, until the liquid reduces by about 1 cup of molasses. Remove from heat. The syrup will continue to thicken as it cools. After the syrup cools completely, store it in an airtight jar or container in the refrigerator for up to 4 weeks.

Bharat
Combine the cinnamon, nutmeg, all spice, black peppercorns, galangal, and clove. Mix together thoroughly.

Continues on page 9

WINE PAIRING FIRESTONE RIESLING 2015, Santa Ynez Valley, CA. A dish with this amount of spicy flavors needs something sweet to off-set the heat. Riesling is known to pair well with dishes that have a bit more heat. This one in particular, adds a touch of Gewürztraminer to give it a bit more sweetness. The Gewürztraminer also adds a bit of Lychee flavor to a wine already hinting green apple, lemon, and peach. These flavors should pair quite nicely with the Bharat.

"Gewürztraminer" in German means "spiced" traminer. Traminer is an ancient German grape varietal..

BHARAT SPICE MIX "Bharat", which means "spice mixture", is the basic spice combination used to flavor some of the most well-known Levantine dishes. For the best flavor, buy the spices whole and grind them yourself. Bharat should be stored in an airtight glass jar in a freezer.

Blue Plate

Vietnamese Meatballs

MEATBALLS
- 1½ pork shoulder
- 2 eggs, lightly beaten
- 3 slices of bacon
- 1 Tbsp dried spearmint
- ¼ cup basil
- 3 Tbsp ginger, peeled and roughly chopped
- 2 Tbsp garlic, whole cloves
- 3 Tbsp cilantro, roughly chopped
- ¾ Tbsp chili flakes
- 1 cup panko crumbs
- 2½ Tbsp sesame seeds
- 5¼ Tbsp heavy cream
- 3½ Tbsp bansankan (eel coating sauce)
- 2¼ Tbsp soy sauce
- 1 Tbsp sugar
- 1 Tbsp distilled vinegar
- 1 Tbsp kosher salt

SAMBAL SOY REDUCTION
- ½ cup brown sugar
- ½ cup soy sauce
- ½ cup distilled vinegar
- ¼ cup sambal sauce (store bought)
- ¼ cup honey

Meatballs
Place eggs, panko crumbs, and heavy cream aside. Toss the remaining ingredients together until well-combined — pork shoulder, bacon, dried spearmint, basil, ginger, garlic, cilantro, chili flakes, sesame seeds, Bansankan (eel coating sauce), soy sauce, sugar, vinegar, and Kosher salt. Run mixture through a small dye on a meat grinder.

Fold eggs, panko, and heavy cream into the seasoned meat mixture. Scoop a small amount of the mixture using a small ball scoop or hands; wet with cold water to reduce sticking. Form into meatballs and place on a baking pan, slightly separated. Bake in a 400 degree oven for 12 minutes.

Sambal Soy Reduction
Combine the brown sugar, honey, soy sauce, distilled vinegar, Sambal, and honey in a small saucepan. Gently warm over medium heat until sugar and honey are fully dissolved and reduce by 25%.

NOTES FROM CHEF When my wife and I visited Vietnam, we ate. And ate. And ate. The flavors used in Asia are so unlike anything we're used to in America. In every dish, there's a complex mixture of sweet and savory, fresh and robust, hot and cold. Every meal was a short story of discovery — literally, we often couldn't read the menu and didn't know what we were ordering. This recipe combines my favorite flavors from that trip into little balls of heaven.

WINE PAIRING HAY MAKER SAUVIGNON BLANC 2017, Marlborough, New Zealand. I find a New Zealand Sauvignon Blanc tends to have too much of a Jalapeño flavor to it so I usually steer away from them. This producer however has made a wine that gives off flavors of lemon, pear, pineapple, and a hint of Green Bell Pepper. The pineapple and pear make an excellent addition to this dish, they help off-set the chili flakes and cilantro quite nicely. The tropical flavors will help round out the dish along with the dried spearmint that the recipe calls for.

SAMBAL An Indonesian chili sauce or paste typically made from a mixture of a variety of chili peppers with secondary ingredients such as shrimp paste, garlic, ginger, shallot, scallion, palm sugar, and lime juice.

Lamb Shank "Shakria" with Yogurt Sauce

LAMB SHANK
4 lamb shanks
1½ gallon water or vegetable stock
4 bay leaves
15 cloves
1 tsp cinnamon
1½ Tsp cardamom
1½ Tbsp Syrian spice (Bharat recipe–pg 4)
4 Tbsp kosher salt
1 tsp white peppercorn
2 large white onions, cleaned and whole

YOGURT SAUCE
3 cups plain Greek yogurt, full fat
1½ cups onion stock
1½ Tbsp cornstarch, dissolved in ½ tsp water

GARNISH
dried spearmint
toasted pistachios
pomegranate seeds

SIDES
rice
favorite vegetable

Lamb Shank
In a large pot, combine lamb shanks, water or vegetable stock, bay leaves, cloves, cinnamon, cardamom, Syrian spice, kosher salt, white peppercorn, and white onions. Bring to boil, then reduce heat and simmer until tender, about 3 hours.
To test doneness, pierce the meat with a wooden skewer. When there is no resistance, it's ready.

Onion Stock
Puree onions with enough lamb broth to achieve a smooth consistency (thicker than broth) and produce 1½ cups onion stock for yogurt sauce.

Yogurt Sauce
Whisk yogurt in a non-reactive pot. Add onion stock and cornstarch (dissolved in ½ tsp water). Whisk until well incorporated. Place pot with yogurt mixture over medium heat. Using a wooden spoon, stir clockwise until the mixture begins to boil. Boil and stir for 3-4 minutes. Remove from heat. Add more kosher salt, Syrian spice (see Bharat recipe on page 4), and cardamom, to taste.

Assembly
Dip lamb shanks in yogurt sauce. Serve with rice and your favorite vegetable. Drizzle with extra yogurt sauce and sprinkle with dried spearmint, pomegranate seeds and toasted pistachios.

Serves 4.

NOTES FROM CHEF *Nothing warms the soul in winter like slow cooked Colorado Lamb. My mother used to make me this dish in Syria when I was young. As the spices dance with the lamb and sing to the yogurt, the flavors seem to crescendo. Then, the dried spearmint, roasted nuts and pomegranate seeds make your mouth fall in love. In my homeland of Levant we are famous for our hot yogurt sauces and soups – which is what sets this recipe apart from other regions that cook lamb. Yogurt can be a little finicky when made hot, so the addition of cornstarch is a must. The memory of adding extra spearmint to my plate as a small child is intertwined with this unforgettable mix of flavors.*

WINE PAIRING PRAGER Wachstum Bodenstein Grüner Veltliner Smaragd (Wachau Austria) 2015. Austria makes some of the best Grüner Veltliners in the world. Franz Prager is one of the highly respected and reputable producers from this region. The aromas give off a vibrant mix of herbs, wildflowers, and a bit of ripe fruit. The term "Smaragd" is a designation of the ripeness for dry wines coming from the Wachau region.

Blue Plate
Feather Ribs with Pickled Jalapenos

RIBS
12 racks of feather ribs (riblettes)

BLUE PLATE RUB
8 oz brown sugar
½ cup kosher salt
½ cup Turkish oregano
½ cup dark chili powder
½ cup cumin
4 Tbsp smoked paprika (Spanish)
½ cup coriander, whole, finely ground
4 Tbsp fennel seed, whole, finely ground
3 star anise
1 can Dr Pepper®
1 can Coca Cola

PICKLED JALAPENOS
1 yellow onion, cut into rings
3 carrots, peeled, sliced on an angle, ¼ inch
10 jalapenos, quartered lengthwise
1 tsp cumin
1 bay leaf
1 tsp Turkish oregano (Mexican is too bitter)
¼ tsp tumeric
2 large cloves garlic, slightly smashed
2 Tbsp canola oil
1½ cup white balsamic vinegar
3 cups distilled vinegar, 50 grain
4 Tbsp Kosher salt
2½ cup water

Blue Plate Rub
Finely grind the coriander and fennel seeds. In a large bowl, mix in the brown sugar, kosher salt, Turkish oregano, dark chili powder, cumin, smoked paprika (Spanish), coriander, fennel seed, and star anise. Completely rub ribs with spice mix.

Ribs
I use feather ribs, (riblettes or tenderloin ribs). My rule of thumb for any tough cuts of meat is 3 hours at 300 degrees. Although, beef brisket (5-6 hours for brisket) has never heard of my rule of thumb most ribs have. I cold smoke my ribs for 1½ hours at 150 degrees. Place ribs in a shallow pan, pour the Dr. Pepper and Coca Cola over the ribs then cover with parchment paper and foil. Increase the oven to 300 degrees. Continue cooking for 3 hours. To check doneness, push a wooden skewer into the meat, it should offer no resistance and be soft, but not falling apart.

Pickled Jalapenos
Sauté garlic in canola oil for 2-3 minutes. In a stainless steel pot add the water, cumin, bay leaf, Turkish oregano, tumeric, sautéed garlic, white balsamic vinegar, distilled vinegar, kosher salt, bring to a boil. When a boil is achieved, add yellow onion rings, carrot slices, and jalapeno strips. Cook for 5-10 minutes, stirring regularly. Strain vegetables out of the vinegar mixture and let cool enough to place in sanitized pickle jars. At the same time, bring your liquid back up to a boil and carefully ladle into the jar with the vegetables. Cover the jars while still hot to seal.

NOTES FROM CHEF *I am often asked what kind of cuisine I serve at my restaurant, and my response is Americana! I think of this as the food that has been brought here by immigration and has evolved into what we eat today in America. Hot dogs are German, pot roast is English, and corned beef and cabbage from the Emerald Isle. The American palate has changed over the years. Until several years ago the number one selling condiment was ketchup. Now it's salsa. But to me, slow cooked ribs with your favorite sauce or no sauce will always be very American. My ribs are a little sweet (ahem, unlike me), so I like to serve them with spicy taqueria pickled jalapenos. I was introduced to these pickles when I moved to La Jolla, CA, in the late 1990's, and it's been a love affair ever since.*

WINE PAIRING *STONE CAP CABERNET 2015, Columbia Valley, Washington. Boasting a vibrant, richer, flavor profile of black cherry, raspberry, currants, toasted oak, chocolate, and spice. My research on this wine states that Ribs are the perfect pairing. The stunning amount of flavors that Blue Plate dishes have call for wines that allow for more layers to be brought forward. Rich, bold fruit flavors are the perfect "ying", to the dishes "yang".*

Blue Plate

Palisade Peach Marmalade

PEACH MARMALADE
5 lbs peaches, blanched and cooked at low simmer for 1½ to 2 hours
5 cups granulated sugar
2 lemons, juiced
4½ tsp kosher salt
1 star anise

Peach Marmalade

In a 1 gallon non-reactive pot, place blanched peaches (see recipe below) and granulated sugar, kosher salt, star anise, and lemon juice. Cook slowly until boiling. Simmer for an additional 40 minutes, constantly stirring so as not to scorch the peaches.

Pre-heat convection oven to 200 degrees with low fan.

Pour the cooked marmalade into non-reactive pan (casserole dish). Place in an oven with a convention fan for 6 hours, if possible. The convection oven does the trick, but, If you don't have one, just use a regular oven for a little longer than my instructions below.

Blanch Peaches

Since it is a quick process to blanch peaches, it helps to have a cutting board, slotted spoon, and bowl of ice water ready to use. Select peaches that are a little soft and fragrant. If you're using peaches that are completely hard, they won't blanch easily. If you want to peel hard peaches, use a Y peeler to remove the skin.

Fill a large pot of water and place on stove. While the water is warmed to a boil, cut an X about 2 inches long through the skin on the bottom of each peach. Scoring the skin of the peaches will make it easier to remove the peel once you've blanched them.

Place peaches into the boiling water for 30 to 60 seconds. The peaches should be submerged. For firm peaches, use the full 60 seconds; for riper peaches, use less time. Avoid leaving peaches in the boiling water for longer as they will overcook.

With a slotted spoon transfer the peaches quickly into the ice bath for 10 seconds (until the skins are cooled) to stop them from cooking. Remove peaches from the ice water. Locate the X on the bottom of each peach and use your fingers to pull off the skins.

NOTES FROM CHEF *When I was younger, my family grew fruit in orchards, under the hot Damascus sun, similar to that of Palisade, CO. Every year, my mother and her friend Mariam Dardoush would make jam in the same manner as this recipe. However, they would place muslin cloth on the cooked jam in wide but shallow pots and place them on our balcony to sit in the sun for a couple of days and dehydrate. The jam would reduce in quantity but grow in flavor. Unfortunately, I can't leave my jam outside due to health issues and Colorado's wildlife. I have personally seen bears outside my restaurant and home, and I'm sure they would love this sweet treat.*

WINE PAIRING *Domino Chardonnay NV, California. This crisp and creamy Chardonnay is pleasantly surprising to the palate. With the rich flavor profile of this dish, the Domino Chardonnay should help balance the richness. The mild citrus tones this wine gives off will help give a bit of acid to the dish making it not feel too heavy. In addition, the other flavors of apricot, honey, and pear will give the dish more texture and flavors of a mixed fruit instead of just the peaches.*

 Harak Isbaao

Harak Isbao, con't from page 4

Crispy Onions
Heat canola oil in saute pan. On medium heat saute one french cut onion for two hours until crispy. Let cool on paper towel.

Garlic & Cilantro
Add chopped garlic to cold oil in saute pan. Turn heat to high, stirring constantly. Once garlic is slightly colored, add cilantro. Be careful of oil splatter. Saute until cilantro is wilted, 1-2 minutes, stirring constantly.

Fried Pita
Cut the pita into 1½ inch squares. Heat canola oil in saute pan. Place pita in pan and fry for 2 minutes until crispy.

Assembly
Layer the lentils and pasta, crispy onions, garlic, and cilantro with the pita.

Garnish with pomegranate seeds.

NOTES FROM CHEF *When the staff at my restaurant called this dish Syrian nachos, I could almost feel my ancestors rolling over in their graves. Understandably (I suppose), this dish is a little unusual for those not accustomed to traditional Syrian foods. You would not see this at a restaurant; instead, it is made in the home and shared with friends and family. The flavors are vibrant, sultry, and I think truly exemplify the old traditions of my homeland.*

GESSNER AT HOTEL TALISA

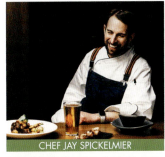

CHEF JAY SPICKELMIER

Mountains inspire every aspect of Hotel Talisa's cuisine. Food and drink celebrate the culinary heritage of Vail Colorado, designed after Swiss and Austrian villages in the European Alps. This inventive blend of cultures echo Vail's own heritage in Gessner, the hotel's premier restaurant.

The restaurant's namesake, Conrad Gessner, was regarded as the father of modern scientific bibliography, zoology, and botany. He was frequently the first to describe a species of plant or animal in the alpine landscapes surrounding Zurich, Switzerland from 1516-1565. Much like Gessner's excursions, we tempt you to take a journey of your senses. Explore the flavors of our alpine-inspired menus that draw upon Vail's European roots and blend locally sourced ingredients, globally inspired techniques, and uniquely curated preparations. We partner with local farms for our vegetables and livestock as well as have their talented staff create some of our cutting boards and service wares from wood derived from the local trees.

"Talisa", translated as "beautiful water" in Ute Indian, showcases a view of Vail mountain and the Gore Creek, framed by floor-to-ceiling windows. In the summer, the accordion doors fold back to reveal an open-air dining experience, and in the winter, our outdoor fire pits invite guests to congregate and create warm moments worth collecting.

Finding his passion and entrepreneur spirit, Chef Spickelmier was at the helm in the kitchen early in his career. In 2001, he began working the gamut of restaurants in the Vail Valley including The Vail Cascade Resort, The Left Bank, The Ritz Carlton, and the Sonnenalp Hotel. After leaving the Vail Valley to bring several restaurant concepts to life in his home town of Denver, he returned in 2011, and joined the Cascade Resort now Hotel Talisa. Jay became the Executive Chef for Hotel Talisa in 2018.

"My passion for cooking is found in the adventurous Rocky Mountain lifestyle, and all that Vail and the surrounding area has to offer. I consider myself an outdoor enthusiast and enjoy everything under the sun. Finding new inspiration to define Rocky Mountain Cuisine only requires a quick glance at the natural beauty that surrounds us."

WINE PAIRINGS *Gessner Sommelier Adam Lewis*

Smoked Trout Deviled Eggs

EGG YOLK FILLING
2 lbs egg yolks
1 cup mayonnaise
3 Tbsp mustard
4 Tbsp cream cheese
½ Tbsp hot sauce
¼ cup cornichons
7 oz smoked trout

1 Tbsp paprika
¼ cup chives
1 Tbsp preserved lemon
2 tsp lemon oil

EGG WHITE BASE
2 lbs egg whites
1 Tbsp salt

PRESERVED LEMON
(can be store bought)
3-5 lemons
¼ cup sugar
2 Tbsp kosher salt
mason jar

Egg Yolk Filling
Separate egg yolks and pour into a baking dish, cover and bake for 25-30 minutes at 350 degrees. Set aside to cool. Set aside a small amount of smoked trout for garnish. Once the egg yolks have cooled, mix together the remaining trout, mayonnaise, mustard, cream cheese, hot sauce, cornichons, paprika, chives, preserved lemon, and lemon oil - Mix well. Press through a tamis (sieve). Should yield 1 quart of filling.

Egg White Base
Pour egg whites into a standard large Pyrex® baking or casserole dish. Cover with food safe plastic wrap* and place in a 350 degree oven for 18-20 minutes. (egg whites coagulate at a temperature of 136 degrees). After the whites set, let stand for 10 minutes before placing in a cooler to drop below 41 degrees. Punch out rounds for the base of each deviled egg.

Preserved lemons
Wash the lemons. Keeping the lemon attached at the bottom, cut into quarters. Sprinkle the insides with the salt and sugar. Squeeze as many of the lemons in the jar until juice seeps up to the top. Add more juice and salt and sugar then close the jar. Rotate the jar regularly over 3 weeks. Wash off salt before using.

Assembly
Place egg whites on your preferred plate. Pipe filling on top and garnish with a little reserved trout or perhaps a little caviar of your choice.

DRINK PAIRING SMOKEY SAZERAC *Rinse a chilled rocks glass with absinthe, discarding any excess into a sink and set the glass to the side. In a mixing glass, muddle 1 sugar cube, 1 tablespoon of water, 3 dashes Peychaud Bitters and 2 dashes Angostura Bitters. Add 1.5 oz. 10th Mountain Rye Whiskey, and 1 oz. Laphroaig Scotch. Fill with ice and stir until well chilled. Strain into the prepared glass. Twist a slice of orange peel over the surface to extract the oils and then discard. Serving Suggestion: Skewer a fresh orange peel around a Luxardo cherry and lay across the top of the rocks glass to garnish.*

*PLASTIC WRAP IN THE OVEN? *We asked the same question. Please note, restaurants use professional grade plastic wrap which has a different chemical composition than typical retail wraps.*

TAMIS *is a flat sieve, similar to the top of a drum but with a mesh.*

Butternut Squash Soup

BUTTERNUT SQUASH SOUP
1½ butternut squash roasted (approx. 8 lbs)
5 garlic cloves
4 jalapeño peppers, seeded
¼ cup ginger, diced
3 yellow onion, diced
½ bottle white wine
1 gallon water
2 qts coconut milk
5 leaves basil
10 limes, zested, juiced
salt and pepper to taste

GARNISH
4 Tbsp coconut milk
2-3 sprigs cilantro

Preheat the oven to 350 degrees.

Butternut Squash Soup
Cut squash in half. Place face down in a baking dish large enough so that squash halves are not touching. Pour water into dish to approximately 1 inch to steam the squash. Bake the squash halves at 350 degrees for about 30 minutes, or until soft and golden in color.
Press the cooked pulp through a screen and cool until ready to finish soup.
Dice the garlic, jalapeño peppers, ginger, and yellow onion.
Place diced garlic, jalapeño peppers, ginger, yellow onion, and white wine into a large kettle, cook on medium heat until translucent. Add the squash puree, water, coconut milk, lime juice and zest, and basil to the kettle.
Simmer on medium heat until blended together. For the final step, in a blender, blend the soup into a smooth purée. Season with salt and pepper to taste.

Garnish
Garnish with swirl of coconut milk and cilantro.

BEER PAIRING VAIL BREWING COMPANY "Hot Mess Blonde" Owner/Brewer Garrett Scahill ABV 5.4% | SRM 4 | IBU 20.
Let's not over complicate this one...it is exactly as it sounds. Smooth, somewhat sweet, slightly malty, and paired with mellow citrus on the nose. "Hot Mess" may come off as a state of bubbly disarray, but this brew still maintains an undeniable attractiveness as our go-to light beer.

BEER SERVING SUGGESTION Have one before the soup, with the soup, and after the soup for maximum effectiveness.

Braised Colorado Lamb Shank, Brussel Sprouts, Lemon Miso Carrots, Parsnip Puree, and Golden Raisin Gastrique

THE LAMB SHANK
6 lamb foreshanks
½ cup of extra virgin olive oil
2 celery stalks, 2-inch slices
2 carrots, 2-inch slices
1½ large onions, cut in ⅛
1 cup tomato paste
3 cups red wine
2 cups white wine vinegar
2 cups Sprite®
7 sprigs of fresh thyme
3 sprigs of fresh rosemary
3 bay leaves
12 cloves of garlic
2 cups demi-glace
1 tsp whole peppercorns
1 tsp sugar
2 qts chicken stock
salt and pepper for seasoning
18 Brussels sprout - 2-3 per person

PARSNIP PURÉE
4 parsnips, cut into medium chunks
1 shallot, diced
4 garlic cloves, finely chopped
2 cups heavy cream
2 cups milk
1 stick of butter (½ cup)
salt and white pepper to taste

BABY CARROTS IN LEMON-MISO GLAZE
18 baby carrots, or 2-3 whole carrots per person
1 cups honey
½ cup extra virgin olive oil
¼ cup freshly minced garlic
5 lemons, zested
2 oz lemon juice
2 Tbsp white miso paste

GOLDEN RAISIN GASTRIQUE*
1 shallots, diced
2 cups golden raisins
1 tsp garlic, minced
2 sprigs of rosemary
5 sprigs of thyme
1 cup white wine
2 cups apple cider vinegar
2 tsp whole grain mustard
1 cup honey
¼ cup sugar
2 tsp lemon juice

Lamb Shank
Preheat the oven to 250 degrees.
Place a baking pan large enough to hold lamb shanks into the oven while it preheats.
Season the lamb shanks with salt and pepper, sear in a large hot pan until golden brown - about 5 minutes on each side. Remove lamb shanks from the pan, place in a dutch oven or in a braising pan and set aside.
Coat the bottom of a medium-sized sauce pan using some of the fat rendered from the lamb shanks; discard the remainder. Add the celery, carrot, and onion. Cook over medium heat until the vegetables are soft and lightly browned, around 6 to 8 minutes.

Continues on page 19

WINE PAIRING MUGA RESERVA *Tempranillo, (Rioja, Spain).*
A wine with black-cherry red and garnet hues. First, red-fruit notes appear on the nose, with hints of fennel and scrubby heartland, all nicely balanced by smoky aromas from the time spent in medium-toasted wood. Underlying hints of vanilla come through with coffee notes. On the palate, there is a full mouth-feel with slightly mentholated nuances and white chocolate. The vanilla reappears and the red-berry fruit aromas found on the nose persist, with an elegant acidity which makes the aftertaste long.

Braised Colorado Lamb Shank, Brussel Sprouts, Lemon Miso Carrots, Parsnip Puree, and Golden Raisin Gastrique

Braised Colorado Lamb Shank, con't from page 18 Add the tomato paste and cook for 3 more minutes, stirring frequently to keep the paste from burning on the bottom of the pan.

Add the red wine, thyme, rosemary, bay leaf, garlic, demi-glace, peppercorns, and sugar. Increase the heat to high and bring to a boil. Cook for about 5 minutes to cook off some of the alcohol. Add the chicken stock, white wine vinegar and Sprite®, stir to combine. Pour mixture over the lamb shanks in the Dutch oven or braising pan. Cover and place into the 250 degree oven. Cook for approximately 5 hours. Timing will vary slightly depending on the size of the lamb shanks. The meat will easily pull off the bone when fully cooked.

Remove the shanks from the Dutch oven or braising pan and set aside for final assembly. Strain the liquid, discarding the solids. Skim any fat that rises to the surface. Set aside.

Brussels Sprout

Split the Brussels in half, season with olive oil, salt and pepper. Roast the Brussels in the oven for approximately 18 minutes or tender and golden.

Parsnip Purée

Peel and cut the parsnips into small 1-2 inch chunks.

Add the shallot, garlic, cream, milk, and parsnips to a pan and bring to a simmer. Cook until the parsnips are tender. Strain and reserve the liquid.

Purée the cooked parsnips in a blender, adding the reserved liquid a small amount at a time as necessary to achieve a silky-smooth consistency.

Pass through a chinois* or fine strainer and season to taste with salt and pepper.

Baby Carrots in Lemon-Miso Glaze

Place the honey in a sauce pan and lightly cook over low heat until caramelized. Remove from heat. Add olive oil, garlic, lemon zest and juice, and miso. Stir to combine. Transfer to a bowl and set aside.

Golden Raisin Gastrique*

Place the shallot, garlic, and raisins in a saucepan. Sweat the mixture by heating gently and stirring frequently until the shallots are tender and slightly translucent.

Add the white wine and simmer to cook off the alcohol. Add all remaining ingredients – vinegar, mustard, honey, sugar, lemon juice, rosemary and thyme. Bring to a boil, then reduce the heat to achieve a gentle simmer.

Cook to reduce the mixture to the consistency of maple syrup. The gastrique is done when it sticks to the back of a spoon.

Assembly

Place the lamb shanks in the oven at 200 degrees for about 10 minutes, or until the bone is hot and the lamb has crisped up a bit. Toss the carrots into the lemon miso-glaze to fully coat.

When ready to serve, spoon the parsnip purée onto the center of the plate and spread into a circle. Place the Brussel sprouts, and carrots onto the puree followed by a lamb shank. Drizzle the golden raisin gastrique over the top and serve.

Add the red wine, vinegar, Sprite®, thyme, rosemary, bay leaf, garlic, demi-glace, peppercorns, and sugar that was put aside. Increase the heat to high and bring to a boil. Cook for about 5 minutes to cook off some of the alcohol.

---

*GOLDEN RAISIN GASTRIUQE *After cooking it will become a simple syrup made from the mixture of the fruit, wine and vinegar. The final product has a maple syrup consistency with sweet tart flavors.*

*CHINOIS *is a cone shaped strainer with a fine mesh. This is the perfect tool to strain purees, soups, and sauces creating a very smooth texture. A Chinois is also perfect to dust food with powdered ingredients.*

Ratatouille

RATATOUILLE
1 medium yellow onion
2 Tbsp garlic, chopped
3 Roma tomatoes, thinly slice
1 Tbsp thyme, chopped
1 Tbsp parsley, chopped
1 can tomato paste
1 Tbsp basil, chopped
1 Tbsp crushed red pepper
2 Tbsp blended oil

VEGETABLE LAYERS
1 yellow squash, thinly slice
1 Japanese eggplant, thinly slice
3 Roma tomatoes, thinly slice
1 zucchini, thinly slice
1 Tbsp extra virgin olive oil
1 oz red sauce

Ratatouille Sauce
Add the blended oil to a medium saute pan, on medium to high heat until hot. Add the chopped onion and cook, stirring occasionally, until translucent. Add the garlic and tomatoes and cook for about another 5 minutes. Add tomato paste and heat to cook out the bitterness, to taste. Stir the chopped thyme, parsley, basil, and crushed red pepper into the sauce. Set aside for service to finish ratatouille.

Vegetables
Thinly slice the zucchini, Japanese eggplant, tomato, and yellow squash.
Coat the bottom of a medium size-muffin mold with extra virgin olive oil.

Assembly
Place the ratatouille sauce in the bottom of the mold. Layer the squash, eggplant and zucchini on top of the ratatouille sauce in the pan. Cover with foil and bake for 15 minutes at 350 degrees. Cool down and serve warm.

DRINK PAIRING *"THE ROOT DOWN" In a mixing glass, combine ½ oz Honey, 3 oz Beet juice, 1 oz Orange and stir until honey is blended into the juices. Fill with ice and add 1½ oz June Creek Gin and 1 oz Domaine de Canton Ginger Liqueur. Shake until completely blended and strain into a coupe glass. Finish with a splash of soda water.*

Coconut Flan

WV | D

FLAN
3 14 oz cans sweetened condensed milk
1 14 oz can unsweetened coconut milk
1 12 oz can evaporated milk
6 large eggs, at room temperature
1 Tbsp vanilla extract
½ tsp salt
½ cup shredded sweetened coconut, toasted
vegetable oil cooking spray

DARK CARAMEL (option 1)
2 cups sugar

DARK CARAMEL (option 2)
2 cups sugar
½ cup water
1 cup heavy whipping cream

Preheat the oven to 350 degrees.

Spray a 10-cup bundt or tube pan with vegetable oil cooking spray. Set aside to prepare caramel and flan.

Dark Caramel (option 1)
In a large, heavy stainless steel skillet, cook 2 cups of sugar over medium until fragrant and begins to melt around edges of pan, about 6 minutes. Gently swirl pan to melt the granulated sugar and continue swirling the pan until all of the sugar has melted and darkened to the color of dark brown sugar. This should take about 10 minutes. Immediately pour melted sugar into prepared pan, coating the bottom evenly. Let stand until cool, about 20 minutes.

Dark Caramel (option 2)
Combine sugar and ½ cup water in heavy deep medium saucepan. Stir over medium heat until sugar dissolves. Increase heat and bring syrup to boil, occasionally brushing down sides of pan with wet pastry brush. Boil without stirring until syrup turns dark amber color, swirling pan occasionally (about 13 minutes). Remove from heat and add cream (mixture will bubble up). Stir caramel until smooth. Caramel sauce can be made 3 days ahead. Transfer to microwave-safe bowl. Cool. Cover and chill. Rewarm in microwave in 15-second intervals before using. Pour the dark caramel on the bottom of the prepared pan. Let it harden and cool.

Flan
Using an electric mixer, beat the milks, eggs, vanilla extract, and salt until smooth. Pour the mixture into a bundt or tube pan. Place the pan inside a large roasting pan. Fill the roasting pan with enough water to come halfway up the sides. Cover the Bundt or tube pan with foil. Bake until the center jiggles slightly when pan is moved, about 1 hour 40 minutes. Remove from the oven and let cool at room temperature for 30 minutes. Refrigerate, covered, for 3 hours or overnight. Pour the dark caramel on the bottom of the plate. Let it harden and cool.

Turn the flan out onto a platter on top of the caramel sauce.

DRINK PAIRING *HOT PEAR CIDER*
Pour Tuaca, ½ oz spiced apple cider mix and ½ oz pear purée in a footed glass mug. Fill with hot water and stir until all ingredients are thoroughly mixed.

SERVING SUGGESTION *Punch 2 cloves into a thin slice of pear, top with a dollop of caramel and cinnamon stick. Rest this garnish on the rim, which looks beautiful as well as retaining the heat of the beverage.*

HARVEST

We live in a world where we are constantly connected. But not always in the way we'd like to be. Too often are we unable to slow down, unwind, and find time for the connections that really matter. Family. Friends. Beautiful shared experiences with loved ones. Those small moments that weave themselves together to create lasting memories.

Harvest Restaurant & Bar is dedicated to creating those moments and cultivating those special memories. Situated beyond the Vail Valley's villages and resorts, Harvest is a place that feels away from it all, yet still like home. It is a place where wholesome, homestyle fare is complemented by stunning mountain views. It is a place where guests are invited to make time for those connections that really matter.

Harvest sets your dining experience amidst postcard-like panoramas from our dining room and expansive patios. The result is more than just a dining experience: Harvest Restaurant & Bar is your Vail Valley home for creating lasting memories. Harvest is casual, comfortable, and consistently excellent. Always fresh, always fun, and always excited to meet our next first-time guest.

One of the very special facets of our restaurant's atmosphere and personality, is that Harvest can be whatever you need it to be. Whether it's a romantic dinner with your special someone, a fun family meal with the kids, drinks and appetizers with your golfing foursome, or the perfect setting for a breathtaking mountain wedding reception. Harvest is each and all of these things at the same time!

Harvest Restaurant & Bar is located in Edwards, CO in the Sonnenalp Club and is part of the Sonnenalp family of businesses. Under the ownership of the Faessler family, the Sonnenalp Club has been a centerpiece of the Singletree community for over 30 years. Harvest upholds the Feassler's commitment to offering the highest quality customer service.

We're looking forward to welcoming you to Harvest.

CHEF ROSA PROVOSTE

Harvest proudly features the New American cuisine of Chilean Executive Chef Rosa Provoste.

Chef Rosa grew up cooking alongside her mother, and fishing and hunting with her father. After starting culinary school at the young age of 14, Chef Rosa's reputation rose as she perfected her craft around the world including resorts in Vanuatu, Cook Islands in the South Pacific, *Santiago, Chile and London, England* and then here in the USA. She stresses only the freshest locally farmed ingredients in her preparations, adding her signature hint of her international background with her time-tested favorites to create her dishes at Harvest.

SHRIMP BRUSCHETTA

POACHED SHRIMP
1 qt peeled and deveined 21/25 size shrimp
2 garlic clove, chopped
1 spring thyme fresh, chopped
1 tsp black pepper freshly cracked
1 lemon, roughly cut
1 bay leaf
1 cup white wine
2 cups water

AVOCADO PURÉE
2 ripe avocado
¼ cup fresh basil leaves
1 lemon, juiced
2 tbsp extra virgin olive oil
salt and pepper to taste

TOMATOES
1 cup cherry tomatoes, halved
extra virgin olive oil
salt and pepper to taste
white balsamic vinegar

GARNISH
fresh basil
drizzle lemon oil or extra virgin olive oil
drizzle white balsamic vinegar
baked lavosh, crackers or grilled country bread

Poached Shrimp
Bring 2 cups of water to a boil. Add the white wine, garlic, thyme, cracked black pepper, and bay leaf. Once boiling, drop the shrimp and cook for 3 minutes or until they are pink. Be careful to not overcook.

Avocado Purée
In a blender puree the ripe avocado, fresh basil, lemon juice, olive oil and season with salt and pepper. Reserve mixture in a plastic pipping bag, if possible, for easy plating.

Assembly
Mix the cherry tomatoes in extra virgin olive oil, salt, pepper and a dash of white balsamic vinegar, add the shrimp and serve on a crispy lavosh or toasted country bread. Add a dollop of the avocado puree and serve. Garnish with drizzle of lemon oil or extra virgin olive oil, a drizzle of white balsamic vinegar, and micro greens or fresh basil.

WINE PAIRING FEUDI DI SAN GREGORIO Fiano di Avellino (Southern Italy) 2016. Here is your shellfish dish go to. This wine boasts a flavor profile of fresh chamomile flowers, peach, and candied oranges. This will give a plethora of layers to add to this dish. It will accent the lemon and orange flavors incredibly well. The citrus element of this wine will also help bring the avocado purée with the lemon juice to create a perfect balance for the whole dish.

Gazpacho

GAZPACHO
6 hot house tomatoes
1 cup cherries, pitted
½ cup cucumber, peeled, seeded, chopped
½ cup red bell peppers, seeded, roughly chopped
1 garlic clove
2 Tbsp good quality extra virgin olive oil
¼ cup sherry vinegar

½ cup ice cubes
½ serrano chile
salt and pepper to taste

GARLIC CROUTONS
sourdough bread, sliced thin
extra virgin olive oil
salt and pepper, to taste
garlic oil

Gazpacho

Peel and seed the cucumber, clean the seeds from the red bell pepper. Roughly chop the red peppers and cucumber.
Place the chopped cucumber and red pepper into a blender. Add the hot house tomatoes, pitted cherries, garlic clove, extra virgin olive oil, sherry vinegar, ice cubes, serrano chile salt and pepper to taste. Purrée in the blender. Season to taste with salt and pepper. Serve immediately while still cold.

Garlic Croutons

To make the garlic croutons, use sourdough bread sliced very thin, seasoned with salt and pepper and brushed with garlic oil. Bake for 3-5 minutes or until is crispy with a nice golden color.

WINE PAIRING CHATEAU GASSIER Le Pas du Moine Rosé (Provence, France) 2017. A fantastic producer from the Southern coast of France, boasts some of the best Rosé wine you can get. There is a delicious minerality along with some vibrant and lush flavors of grapefruit and strawberry. With the spice in the Gazpacho this rosé will pair perfectly adding some brightness along with delicious fruit characteristics.

Steamed Mussels with Nduja and Parsley in Saffron broth

MUSSELS
extra virgin olive oil
2 garlic cloves, thinly sliced
1 white onion, thinly sliced
Prince Edward Island Mussels, cleaned and brushed
Roma tomatoes, small diced
Nduja (prosciutto spread)

LOBSTER SAFFRON BROTH
¼ cup olive oil
1 yellow onion, peeled and cut in quarts
2 carrots, peeled and cut in quarts
2 celery stalks
pinch saffron
pinch salt kosher
1 lb mussels, fresh
1 lb clams, fresh
1 lb Maine lobster bodies
1 cup white wine
¼ cup vermouth
¼ cup pernod
1 cup Italian whole peeled tomatoes (with juice)
4 cups vegetable stock

Mussels with Nduja

Preheat a large sauté pan, drizzle in the olive oil. Add the sliced garlic and onion; sweat for a couple of minutes at medium-heat until transparent. Add the prosciutto spread (Nduja), tomatoes and mussels and cook for two more minutes. Add 1 cup of saffron broth and let the liquids reduce by half. Add a cube of butter and mound*. Taste, adjust the seasoning and finally add the parsley and cracked black pepper just before serving.

Lobster Saffron broth

Sweat the onion, carrots, and celery in olive oil until translucent and soft. Add the saffron and toast for two minutes.
Add the mussels, clams and Maine lobster bodies and cook until the mussels and clams release their juice.
Add the white wine, vermouth and pernot, reduce them to au sec (reducing to minimum volume of liquid to maximize the flavor) then add the tomatoes and finally add the vegetable stock. Simmer until it has reduced by a third.
Strain through chinois, bring the temperature down in an ice bath and use as a base for soups, risotto or seafood sauces.

WINE PAIRING DOMAINE LAROCHE , ST. MARTIN, (Chablis, Burgundy, France) 2017. I love a crisp white wine mussels. This Chablis, from Northern Burgundy, is from one of the top producers in the region. With a racy minerality and a hint of fruit this wine will add a pleasant flavor profile to the Saffron and Lobster broth.

NDUJA originates from a small village (Spilinga) in the Monte Poro mountain. Nduja is a pork-based product in which ground pork is kneaded together with salt and calabrian chili pepper. The mixture is then made into sausage by encasing the mixture in the animal's natural intestinal lining.

***MOUND** is a term used when adding chunks of cold butter into a warm or hot mixture. This method of adding butter gives the sauce texture, flavor and a glossy appearance. This is the last step you do before serving.

Harvest
RESTAURANT & BAR

Colorado Lamb Shank with Hand Rolled Potato Gnocchi, Roasted Pumpkin, Green Beans and Sage Brown Butter

LAMB SHANK
10 -16 oz Colorado lamb shanks
2 celery stalks, diced
1 yellow onion, diced
2 large carrots, peeled and diced
1 rosemary sprig
garlic cloves, to taste
2 Tbsp oil blend
4 cups chicken or beef stock
lamb jus

GNOCCHI
1 ⅓ lbs Idaho potato
1 cup Flour
1 egg yolk
1 egg, whole
¼ tsp nutmeg, freshly ground
½ tsp Kosher salt
¼ tsp black pepper, freshly ground
roasted pumpkin (small diced)

VEGETABLES
1 small pumpkin, roasted
1 lb green beans

SAGE BROWN BUTTER
4 Tbsp butter
4-5 sage leaves
½ lemon, juiced

Lamb Shank
In a sauté pan, heat the oil blend and sear the lamb on both sides. Place the seared lamb shanks in a double boiler. Dice the celery stalks and yellow onion. Add the diced carrots, garlic and rosemary sprig, and chopped garlic cloves to the lamb. Pour over chicken or beef stock and cover with a lid or foil. Cook at low-medium temperature for around 4-5 hours, until the meat is tender and you can see the bare bone.

Gnocchi
Pre-heat oven to 350 degrees.
Wash the potatoes thoroughly and put them in a sheet pan. Pinch the potatoes and roast them in preheated oven until cooked through, about 1½ hours.

Take them out of the oven and working very fast, peel them and pass through a food mill or ricer to create a purée.
Transfer the potato purée to a wide pot and dry the purée at low temperature until most of the moisture evaporates. At this point we will add the salt, pepper and nutmeg. Taste and adjust seasoning, if necessary. *Continues on page 32*

WINE PAIRING Chateau Rouget (Pomerol, Bordeaux, France) 2003. Hailing from the right bank of Bordeaux in Pommerol, Chateau Rouget is predominantly a Merlot blend. An aged wine where you will taste some of those Tiertiary flavors with a bit of fruit. Due to the age of this wine the tannins will have softened very elegantly. When younger, Merlot grapes produce more tannin structure due to the thicker skins. This wine gives off flavors of plums, cassis, black truffle, and some wet leaves. The 2003 vintage was considered an off-vintage in comparison to 2000 and 2005 however they are drinking beautifully right now.

ⓔ Colorado Lamb Shank with Hand rolled potato gnocchi (cont'd)

Colorado Lamb Shank, con't from page 31 Transfer the potato purée to a mixing bowl, add the flour and the egg at the same time. Knead with your hands until all the flour is absorbed.
Quickly divide the dough into 4 equal pieces and roll them into thin cylinders.
Cut the potato gnocchi cylinders into small pieces, create the traditional, striped marks on the gnocchi board and place them on a half-sheet tray.
Blanch the pieces in a large pot of boiling salted water until they come up to the surface, approximately one minute.

Sage Brown Butter
Heat a pan and add 4 tablespoons of butter. Once it's melting and smoking add the sage and the lemon juice.
In an oven roasting pan roast the pumpkin.

Vegetables
Dice the pumpkin, drizzle with extra virgin olive oil and roast in the oven for 45 minutes. Sauté the green beans.

Assembly
Toss the gnocchi together with the sautéed green beans and roasted pumpkin and plate. Serve with the lamb shank, top with sage brown butter and serve immediately.

STRAWBERRY-RHUBARB COBBLER

STRAWBERRY-RHUBARB FILLING
4½ cups diced rhubarb
2 cups sliced strawberries
½ cup butter
½ cup sugar
1 tsp orange zest

1 tsp minced fresh ginger
1 oz Kentucky Bourbon
1 Tbsp cornstarch
2 eggs (for egg wash)
pinch of salt

BISCUIT CRUST
1 cup all purpose flour
2 Tbsp sugar
¾ tsp baking powder
½ tsp cinnamon

Strawberry-Rhubarb Filling
Cook the rhubarb with the butter, sugar, orange zest and ginger. Once the rhubarb is soft, add the bourbon. Cook for two minutes then thicken the mixture with the cornstarch.
Add the strawberries and continue to cook for one minute. Cool the mixture.

Biscuit Crust
In mixing bowl add the flour, sugar, baking powder and cinnamon. Mix well into a crumble.

Egg Wash
In a small bowl, beat the egg with a fork. Add a teaspoon or two of water and a pinch of salt. Stir mixture until combined. The egg wash will add a bit of shine and a bit of color, as well as keeping the crumble together.

Assembly
Place the Strawberry-Rhubarb filling mixture into a 6-7oz baking dish. Completely top the fruit mixture with the biscuit crust then brush the surface with the egg wash and bake at 350 degrees for about 8 minutes.

Serves 6-8

WINE PAIRING ZARDETTO PROSECCO (Veneto, Italy). Located in the heart of the region known for Prosecco, between Conegliano and Valdobiadene Iraly, Zardetto has been one of the top producers for over 40 years. What a great pairing for the strawberry-rhubarb cobbler. The intense flavors of orange rind, honeyed grapefruit, and brioche will create a harmonious blend of flavors with this delectable dessert.

JUNIPER RESTAURANT

CHEF MACIAS, ABEL, CHEF OFSANKO

Carving out a niche for a memorable fine dining is Juniper Restaurant, situated along the Eagle River in Riverwalk in Edwards, and minutes from Vail and Beaver Creek. It was in the heart of the Vail Valley that Doug Abel created his dream for a new restaurant with then Executive Chef Todd Bullis in 2002, based on a proven model. "Basically, I wanted a down-valley Sweet Basil, from the minute you walk in the door, all the way through the dining experience," says Abel, referring to Vail's famed fine dining establishment.

Juniper's comfortable ambiance, "is like a city bistro in the mountains", Abel describes. Nothing escapes his attention, from the wine selection to the linen tablecloths to the lighting throughout the main dining room and newly enclosed patio overlooking the Eagle River. Executive Chef Scotty Ofsanko, Chef Santos Macias, and Abel, arrive early in the afternoon, enlivening the place with motivational pats on the backs and helpful observations for the staff.

Color and creativity from plated dish to the dining area, bar, and patio showcase the mastery of Executive Chef Scotty Ofsanko and Chef Santos Macias. Chef Ofsanko, Chef Macias, and Abel collaborate to create their well-known menu of American cuisine with a Western flair. The gentlemen share a passion for fine food made using seasonal, locally sourced ingredients featuring fresh greens and stone fruits in summer to root vegetables in winter. "Made in house" is the foundation of their menu from soups and sauces, to pizza doughs to breads. Whatever the season, Ofsanko and Macias take great care and pride to artfully present a memorable culinary experience to their guests.

Both Chef Macias and Chef Afsanko share a passion for fine food and the process in which it's created and delivered to the guest. They are committed to using only the freshest ingredients that are locally grown (when available) and only products that are in season. Everything is made in-house and from scratch (except angel hair pasta). Their passion is evident and strictly follows the work- hard play-hard mantra as you'll find them on the slopes of Vail and Beaver Creek in the winter and these same trails and others on their mountain bikes in summer.

Santos Macias worked at L'Ostello before moving, in 1994, on to world- renowned Sweet Basil. Training at some of the finest bakeries and restaurants in San Francisco, Santos learned how to develop and operate an extensive bread program. In 2002, he became Chef de Cuisine and Kitchen Manager at Juniper Restaurant.

Scotty Ofsanko, a graduate, in 2001, from John & Wales University in Charleston, SC., became Executive Chef at Juniper in 2013. Scotty worked at the Charleston Place Hotel under James Beard Chef Bob Waggoner, after which continued with, James Beard chef, Enzo Steffanelli, at Sea Island Grille in SC. Next was a Sous Chef position at Budiroes. In November of 2004, Next as Sous Chef at Rocks Modern Grill in Beaver Creek, CO under Chef John Trejo. In 2007, he moved on as Chef de Cuisine at the Vail Plaza Hotel.

Grilled Mediterranean Octopus with Grilled Eggplant, Watercress, Frisee and Romesco Sauce

OCTOPUS
1 Mediterranean octopus
3 cups extra virgin olive oil
8 garlic cloves, smashed
2 oz fresh thyme
2 oz smoked paprika
2 oz Old Bay Seasoning
1 large shallot, rough chopped
1 tsp salt

ROMESCO SAUCE
8 oz roasted Piquillo peppers
3 garlic cloves
½ shallot, rough chopped
1 tsp smoked paprika
½ cup sherry vinegar
1 cup extra virgin olive oil
salt and pepper to taste
1 cup roasted almonds

EGGPLANT and GARNISH
1 eggplant sliced for grilling
1 bunch watercress
1 bunch frissee
1 lemon, juiced
salt and pepper

Romesco Sauce
In a large blender, add the piquillo peppers, garlic cloves, shallot, smoked paprika, and sherry vinegar. Blend until smooth, then slowly add the extra virgin olive oil, season with salt and pepper and finish with roasted almonds.

Octopus
In a large pot, boil enough water add salt and bring water to a boil to blanch octopus for about 10 minutes.
Remove and place in an ice bath, cool and place in vacuum seal bag with the smashed garlic cloves, fresh thyme, smoked paprika, Old Bay Seasoning, and chopped shallot.
Use a food saver to remove remaining air. Place in water and immersion circulator (Sous Vide) to 171.4 degrees and cook for 5 hours. Remove from water and drain liquid. Cool or place on hot grill to char. Once cooked, slice the octopus.

Place cleaned watercress and frissee in a bowl and drizzle extra virgin olive oil, a squeeze of fresh lemon juice and salt and pepper.

Eggplant
Wash and slice the eggplant. Prepare for grilling with a touch of extra virgin olive oil and season with salt and pepper. Then Grill.

Assembly
Place dressed watercress and frissee on a plate.
Place the octopus on top and finish with grilled eggplant, Romesco sauce and roasted almonds.

WINE PAIRING ARGIOLAS "Costera" Cannonau di Sardegna (Sardinia, Italy) 2010. This wine is a delightful pairing to go with this dish. Sardubua, an island off the coast of Italy, is known for some amazing red wines. The Cannonau (Grenache) grape varietal has an intense dark and rich fruit profile. Lots of great flavors of black cherries, ripe strawberries, and a hint of herbs and spice. What a great match for a Romesco sauce as it tends to have a bit of heat and spice.

Potato wrapped Alaskan Halibut with Rock Shrimp-Corn Succotash, Pickled Red Onion & Herb Oil

HALIBUT
1 halibut, whole, Cut into 3 equal pieces
¼ cup of olive oil
2 Yukon Gold potatoes, cut into strings
2 oz pea tendrils (Garnish)

PICKLED RED ONIONS (Garnish)
2 red onions
2 cups red wine vinegar
1 cup water
1½ cups granulated sugar
2 Tbsp salt

BEURRE BLANC
1 tsp extra virgin olive oil
1 lb unsalted butter, cold, cubed
1 oz thyme
4 oz white wine
1 shallot, diced
1 lemon, juiced
salt and pepper to taste

CORN SUCCOTASH
1 tsp extra virgin olive oil
8 oz rock shrimp
4 ears of fresh corn, grilled, cooled and cut off the cob
4 oz fava beans, blanched and cleaned
1 red bell pepper, chopped
2 shallots, diced

HERB OIL
1 cup canola oil
4 oz parsley, chopped
4 oz basil, chopped
4 oz chives, chopped
salt

Pickled Red Onions
Place red onions, red wine vinegar, water, granulated sugar, and salt in a large sauce pan. Simmer until soft until most liquid has evaporated. Refrigerate up to a week.

Herb Oil
Place parsley, basil, chives and canola oil in a blender. Puree until smooth and emulsified. Season with salt and reserve.

Beurre Blanc
In a sauté pan, add the olive oil and sweat the diced shallot until soft. Add the white wine, lemon juice, thyme, and salt and pepper. Reduce liquid by half. Mound in cold, cubed butter slowly, stirring constantly. Strain and reserve in warm place until ready to serve.

Succotash
In a hot pan with oil, add the rock shrimp and season with salt and pepper. Add corn, shallots, fava beans, and red bell pepper, in the pan with shrimp. Sauté until shrimp is cooked through.

Halibut
Cut Halibut into 3 pieces and wrap with Yukon Gold potato strings. In hot pan, heat the olive oil and cook all sides until potato is golden brown and crispy. Finish in oven. Plate on top of succotash. Garnish with pickled onions and pea tendrils. Finish with beurre Blanc. Serves 3.

WINE PAIRING CRAGGY RANGE Te Muna Road, Sauvignon Blanc (Martinborough, New Zealand) 2017. The fresh herbal quality as well as the bright lime acid notes with this wine will create a quintissential pairing for Halibut, a leaner fish with a slight sweet flavor.

Veal Scallopini with Angel Hair 'Caprese', Asparagus, Lemon Beurre Fondue and Veal Reduction

VEAL
1 lb Veal top round (sliced thin and pounded into 3 pieces)
4 oz all-purpose flour
salt and pepper, to taste

VEGETABLES and PASTA
1 bunch asparagus (cut into coin size)
1 pint cherry tomatoes (cut in ½)
1 lemon zest
2 oz basil chiffonade
8 oz angel hair pasta

VEAL DEMI-GLACE
3 lbs veal bones
2 onion, diced
2 carrots, diced
3 celery stalks, diced
4 oz tomato paste
balsamic vinegar, to taste

BEURRE BLANC
1 lb unsalted butter, cubed
1 shallot, diced
1 oz thyme

4 oz white wine
1 lemon
salt and pepper to taste

GARNISH
4 oz fresh mozzarella diced
2 oz fried capers
2 oz veal demi-glace
2 oz beurre blanc
2 oz basil chiffonade

Veal Demi-Glace
Roast veal bones in the oven for 1 hour. Remove from oven, rub with tomato paste, add the diced onions, carrots and celery. Roast for another 30 minutes. Remove bones from the pan and place them in a large pot with water. Simmer bones for 18 hours. Strain and reserve the liquid. Continue cooking to reduce liquid by 80%. Season with salt and pepper and balsamic vinegar.

Beurre Blanc
In a small pan sweat the shallot until soft, then add the white wine, lemon juice, thyme, salt and pepper. Reduce liquid by half. Mound in the cubed butter, slowly, constantly stirring. Strain and reserve in warm place until ready to serve.

Veal
Slice into 3 thin pieces. Pound the veal slices until very thin pieces and season with salt and pepper, then dredge in flour. In a heated pan, sauté the coated veal slices on high heat for 30 seconds on each side. Place on plate.

Vegetables
In a heated sauce pan sauté the asparagus, cherry tomato and finish with basil. In a large pot filled with water, bring to boil and add angel hair pasta. Angel hair pasta will cook quickly so keep watch.

Assembly
Toss vegetables with angel hair pasta and place on top of the veal. Garnish with fried capers, diced mozzarella and torn basil. Top with veal demi-glace and beurre blanc. Serves 3.

WINE PAIRING BOUCHARD PERE & FILS, Beaune Greves, 1er Cru, Vigne de L'Enfant Jesus (Burgundy, France) 2016. An amazing wine to pair with this dish. Bouchard is one of the top producers of Burgundy with some of the best Pinots for countless years. A Pinot with seductive flavors of juicy red berries and a hint of violets. The layers of spice help adding extra flavors to the Demi-glace. The rich plum and dark currants also add to the meat itself and give it a bit of a fruitier flavor.

Juniper RESTAURANT

House Made Butternut Squash Raviolis with Toasted Hazelnuts and Pomegranate Molasses

RAVIOLI FILLING
2 medium butternut squash
1 cup Mascarpone Cheese
½ nutmeg, micro planed
1 oz maple syrup
salt & pepper to taste

3 Tbsp butter

GARNISH
1 oz sage, chiffonade
dried pumpkin flakes
pomegranate molasses (from your local grocer)
pomegranate seeds
sunflower sprouts
toasted hazelnuts, crushed

RAVIOLI DOUGH
½ lb all purpose flour
½ lb semolina flour
5 whole eggs
2 egg yolks
1 ½ tsp salt
½ oz canola oil
1 oz water

Pre-heat oven to 350 degrees.

Ravioli Filling
Peel and cut the butternut squash in half and sprinkle with salt and pepper, roast in the oven at 350 degrees for 1½ hours. Remove from oven, cube squash into pieces and run through a food mill. Add Mascarpone cheese, micro planed nutmeg, maple syrup, and salt and pepper. Place mixture in a pipping bag and reserve for ravioli sheets.

Ravioli Dough
In a large mixing bowl, combine the all purpose flour, semolina flour, and salt. Add eggs, water, and oil slowly and mix with fork until it starts to come together in a ball of dough. Knead by hand for 5 minutes. Wrap in plastic and place in refrigerator to rest for at least 20 minutes.

Ravioli Assembly
If available, use pasta machine and roll out ravioli dough into sheets. With a piping bag, place a strip of the ravioli filling along the middle of pasta sheets, brush with egg yolk wash and fold pasta in half and pinch and form ravioli.
Cut with pasta cutter, place in boiling salted water and cook until the raviolis float.

Sauté Ravioli
Sauté cooked ravioli in pan with sage and butter until golden brown.

Assembly
Place on plate and garnish with pomegranate seeds, pomegranate molasses, pumpkin flake, hazelnuts and sunflower sprouts.

WINE PAIRING AEQUOREA, Spanish Springs Vineyard Vigonier (Central Coast, California) 2017. The Spanish Springs vineyard is located about 2 miles from the Pacific Ocean so it gets the sea air which allows the grapes to have a salinity quality when the wine is produced. The aromatics on this wine are stunning to say the least. With an amazing flavor of white peach, citrus, pineapple, with a great floral finish, this Vigonier, fermented in neutral French Oak and Stainless Steel, has a richness to it..

CHIFFONADE shredded or finely cut leaf vegetables, used as a garnish for soup.

The ORIGINAL Sticky Toffee Pudding Cake
By Charles Broshinsky

PUDDING CAKE
2¼ cups dates (pitted)
2 cups water
2 tsp vanilla
2 tsp baking soda
1 lb all purpose flour

1 tsp baking powder
1 pinch salt
4 oz butter
12 oz sugar
2 whole eggs

TOFFEE SAUCE
4 oz butter
1 lb brown sugar
2 cups heavy cream
2 Tbsp dark rum
or brandy

Pre-heat oven to 325 degrees.

Dates (First Boiling)
Cover the dates with water and bring to boil. Cook for 2 or 3 minutes. Remove and strain. When dates have cooled enough to handle, peel and chop. If you can find pre peeled & chopped dates you can skip this first step and use those instead.

Dates (Second Boiling)
Return the chopped dates to the pan and cover again with the two cups of water. Bring back to a boil then remove from heat and set aside to cool.
Sift the baking powder, flour and salt together.
Cream the butter and sugar then add the eggs. Then add the vanilla. When the dates have cooled a bit, alternate adding part of the dates including liquid, and part of the dry ingredient mixture from above, until all ingredients are in the batter and the batter is smooth.
Spray 4 oz tins with a nonstick spray then scoop the mixture into the tins. Cover with a piece of parchment paper then another tray.

Bake at 325 degrees for approximately 15 minutes. When slightly browned and firm, remove. Let cool and remove from the tins.

Toffee Sauce
Melt the butter and sugar together. Stir in the cream and bring to a full boil. (Use a pan large enough for the sauce to boil up). Remove from heat and let cool a bit before stirring in the rum or brandy.

Assembly
Using the same 4 oz tins, fill the tins about ¼ full with Toffee Sauce then return the puddings to the tins. They may now be kept either in the refrigerator or the freezer for later usage. When ready to serve, remove from the tin and warm in the microwave oven with some additional sauce. Top with your favorite soft whipped cream.

Serves 10, 4 oz portions.

WINE PAIRING *D'OLIVEIRA Madeira Verdelho (Madeira) 1986. D'Oliveira is one of the greatest producers to have survived the Phylloxera era (the disease that killed and destroyed many vineyards throughout Europe). I had the pleasure of having a glass of the 1986 when I visited Gramercy Tavern in New York City – it proved to be an incredible wine.*

With its amazing qualities of mocha, black tea, and a bit of baking spices, this Madeira will be the perfect match for your end of meal treat.

ALTITUDE NOTE *This recipe is adjusted for elevation, approximately 8,000 feet. At sea level, you will need to double the baking powder.*

LA BOTTEGA

La Bottega Restaurant began as a 15 seat restaurant on the outskirts of Vail in 1997. When Stephen and Elisabetta Virion took over the space, they were looking for a niche to fill in Vail. They began with a small deli specializing in East Coast Hoagies and a small menu of pastas, soups and salads. In 1999, they expanded adding a pizza oven, expanding the menu and becoming a full-fledged restaurant. In 2001, they again expanded adding a wine bar. 2006 saw another remodel this name bringing a Tuscan farmhouse look throughout the restaurant and expanding the restaurant capacity and menu.

Prior to La Bottega, Stephen lived in Europe where he met Elisabetta in Vienna. After meeting, they decided to return to the States where Stephen worked in Philadelphia and Chicago. Elisabetta always wanted to go back to Italy, so they moved back to Europe, settling in Tuscany. It was in Tuscany where Elisabetta began working for one of the top wine producers of the region. Here she began what would become her passion for wines. After working for several years in Italy, they made the decision to move to Vail and start their business. With Stephen in the kitchen and Elisabetta in the front, they transformed what was a small corner shop into one of Vail's most established restaurants.

Stephen and Elisabetta have two daughters Stephanie and Valentina. Stephanie has taken over in this family oriented business as General Manager. Valentina is studying neuroscience with her focus is on concussion rehabilitation.

Besides La Bottega, Stephen and Elisabetta own Delizioso Mercato, which reincorporates the deli into a market. They are currently working on their next venture, Barrio Social, which will bring the flavors of Spain to the Vail Valley

CHEF STEPHEN VIRION

Stephen began his career in the restaurant industry at the age of 15. Having always enjoyed cooking since he was quite young, he continued on this path attending the Culinary Institute of America in Hyde Park, N.Y. After working for several years in the States, he decided to broaden his culinary horizons and moved to Europe to work in Zurich, Vienna, Paris and London. In Vienna, he met Elisabetta, who is now his wife and business partner at La Bottega. Elisabetta is from Asiago, Italy.

Bruschetta with Duck Foie Gras and Palisade Peaches

FOIE GRAS
6 3 oz Slices of Duck Foie Gras
6 slices Tuscan bread approximately ½ inch thick and 4 inches across

PEACH SYRUP
4 Colorado Palisade peaches (or other ripe peaches)
4 Tbsp unsalted butter
¼ tsp cinnamon (optional)
dry Italian white vermouth
salt

Grillled Tuscan Bread
Take the sliced bread and grill in a panini machine or under a salamander. If you have neither, place in a toaster.

Peach Syrup
Wash the peaches. They can be peeled or you may leave the skin on based on preference. Slice the peaches using a paring knife into a pan.

Heat 2 tablespoons of the butter in a pan and add the peaches. Do this at the moment you are ready to prepare the peaches. Otherwise, add some lemon juice and a touch of sugar to prevent them from turning brown.

Saute the peaches adding approximately ¼ tsp of cinnamon if you prefer. Add the vermouth and let reduce to ⅓ of the original volume. Add the remaining butter and remove from heat while continuing to swirl the pan.
This will create a syrup for your Bruschetta. Keep warm.

Fois Gras
When ready to serve, season the foie gras slices and place in a very hot cast iron skillet. Sear about one minute on each side depending on the thickness.

Assembly
Place the Foie Gras on top of the grilled bread. Place on plate and top with the peach blend. Take a little of the rendered Foie fat and drizzle over the top if you so desire. Serve immediately.

Serves 6

WINE PAIRING VEUVE CLIQOT Brut Champagne NV (Champagne, France). *If there is one great pairing in the world it is Champagne and Foie Gras. The ever so popular Veuve "Yellow Label" is perfect for this dish. Being a drier champagne this helps to off-set the sweetness of the peach aspect of the dish. Because of the richness of Duck Foie Gras the mineral aspect of this Champagne will also cut through the heaviness of the dish, for a delicious tastebud experience.*

Their Champagne has fantastic flavors of grapefruit and ginger on the palate which will add some additional flavors and layers to the dish as well.

FOIE GRAS VS PATÉ *Paté is a seasoned paste made from ground meat or vegetables. You can find a variety of Paté, from poultry, game, beef, seafood, lamb or pork. Foie Gras is paté made from the fattened liver of geese or ducks.*

Tenderloin of Beef Carpaccio with Parmigiano Reggiano, Organic Arugula and Truffle Cream

BEEF CARPACCIO
24 oz center cut beef tenderloin
   completely trimmed
8 oz organic baby arugula
4 oz Parmigiano Reggiano, shaved

3 lemons, juiced
4 oz extra virgin olive oil
4 oz truffle cream
salt and pepper to taste

TRUFFLE CREAM
3 egg yolks
2 tsp. water
4 oz. truffle oil
salt to taste

Tenderloin

Taking a very sharp knife, cut the tenderloin into very thin slices and place onto plastic wrap laid out onto counter top. Place another sheet of plastic wrap on top and lightly pound the tenderloin to get it as thin as possible without tearing. Place the tenderloin onto chilled plates covering the entire bottom of the plate. Sprinkle the lemon juice onto the meat and distribute over all the meat to "cook" the meat. Season with salt and freshly ground pepper.

Place the organic arugula over top of the meat completely covering the surface. Drizzle the Extra virgin olive oil over the plates and then, using a spoon or small squeeze bottle, distribute the truffle cream over all the plates. Take a potato peeler and shave the Parmigiano Reggiano over top of the plates and serve.

Truffle Cream

In a mixing bowl, place the yolks and water. Slowly drizzle on the truffle oil to form a loose mayonnaise. If too thick, add a bit more water to the mixture. Season with salt.

Serves 6

WINE PAIRING *DOMAINE DES BAGUIERS Bandol Rose, (Cote de Provence, France). This clean and crisp style of rose is the perfect pairing. The acid and the hint of fruit with this wine will bring your palate to life when you try your first bite of this dish. There are subtle hints of candied apple in addition to chalky flavor which to adds a crisp minerality to it. Or to keep it italian, Cleto Chiarli "Vecchia Modena Lambrusco di Sorbara" (Emilia Romagna, Italy)*

La Ribollita, White Tuscan Bean and Vegetable Soup

VEGETABLES
3½ oz extra virgin olive oil
2 Spanish onions, sliced
1 or 2 dried chilies, chopped fine
2 ripe tomatoes; peeled, seeded, coarsely chopped
1 Tbsp tomato puree
1 leek, finely diced
3 celery stalks, finely diced
2 medium carrots, finely diced

2 garlic cloves, crushed
2 rosemary stalks
4 sage leaves
2 bunches red swiss chard
salt and freshly ground white pepper
1 loaf stale bread, sliced

BEAN PURÉE
1 lb dry cannellini beans, soak overnight
1 medium onion, cut into quarters

1 celery stalk
1 medium carrot, peeled, cut into pieces
3 or more garlic cloves
1 sprig rosemary
2 sage leaves
salt

GARNISH
1 onion, diced
extra virgin olive oil

Bean Puree
Soak the cannellini beans overnight in cold water. The next day drain well and place in a heavy casserole dish. Add, medium onion, celery stalk, carrot pieces, garlic cloves, sprig of rosemary, sage leaves and salt to taste.

Cover the bean and vegetable mixture with water, about 2 inches above the top of mixture. Bring to a slow boil. Remove the foam as it rises to the top of the liquid.

When the majority of the foam has been removed, add salt to taste. Let simmer for approximately 4 hours or until the beans are tender. Remove the majority of the beans setting some aside in a large bowl leaving them whole. Place the rest of the mixture into a food mill and puree. Add puree with the whole beans and set aside.

Vegetable Mixture
In a heavy bottom casserole, add the olive oil, sliced onions and dried, chopped chilies and let cook slowly until tender. Add the diced leek, celery stalks, carrots, garlic cloves, rosemary, sage, and red swiss chard and sauté until tender. Next add the tomatoes and tomato puree and cook for several minutes.

Combine the bean puree into the tomato vegetable mixture (it should be fairly runny; if not add more water). Simmer for approximately 2 hours. Stir the pot often to keep from sticking to the bottom. Season with salt and ground white pepper to taste.

Assembly
Let the soup stand overnight. When ready to serve, in the bottom of each soup bowl place a slice of stale bread that has been rubbed with garlic. Then ladle the soup over the bread. The soup can be heated or, typically in Tuscany, it is served room temperature.

Garnish
Garnish with thinly sliced onions with extra virgin olive oil drizzled over the top of the soup.

Serves 6

WINE PAIRING *PAZO CILLEIRO* Albariño (Rias Baixas, Spain) 2017. Albarinos are refreshing wines with a great acidity. This particular one, gives off a fabulous array of aromas; white peach, lychee, lily, and citrus blossom. The soil combination of granite, quartz, give it great structure that keep this wine fresh and alive.

Fettuccine with Jumbo Wild Prawns "Fra Diavolo"

FETTUCCINE
3½ cups Italian 00 flour (or all purpose)
5 medium eggs
¼ tsp salt

PRAWNS FRA DIAVOLO
30 U-12 prawns or shrimp (fresh or frozen)
   peeled and de-veined
3 oz olive oil
½ tsp crushed Italian Peperoncino pepper
   (more or less can be added depending
   on your desired heat level)
5 cloves chopped garlic
1 tsp fresh chopped oregano
¼ cup white wine
2 cups San Marzano tomatoes,
   (or canned), chopped, very ripe
salt and freshly ground pepper, to taste

Fettuccine
Place the flour on a clean, preferably marble or granite, counter top. Form a well in the middle of the flour. Place the eggs and salt in the middle of the well and with a fork, beat as for scrambled eggs. With your hands, slowly blend the flour into the eggs until all the flour is blended in. Knead the dough for about 10 minutes until the mixture is very smooth. Cover with plastic and let rest for a minimum one hour.

Using a pasta machine, make the fettuccine using the fettuccine roller, (if you don't have a fettuccine roller use linguini). Follow the directions for your pasta machine.
Should you not have the time or a pasta machine, use a high quality Italian imported fettuccine. One pound of dry pasta will give you 6 very good-sized portions.

Prawns "Fra Diavolo"
In a skillet, heat the olive oil. When hot, add the garlic and peperoncino, sauté until the garlic is slightly browned. Add the prawns and sauté with the garlic. Remove the shrimp from the pan. Add the white wine and deglaze the pan. Add the tomatoes and oregano. Let the sauce come to a simmer and add the prawns back into the pan. Season with salt. In a large bowl add the cooked pasta and sauce mixing thoroughly.

Cooking Pasta
Bring a gallon of water to a boil. Add enough sea salt so as to make the water taste like the ocean. Add the fresh pasta and cook for 2 minutes then drain in a colander. Toss immediately with "Fra Diavolo" sauce. For dry pasta, follow instructions on package.

Assembly
Remove the prawns and arrange them on the outside of warmed plates. With a pair of tongs, twirl the pasta that has been tossed with the sauce and place in center. Garnish with fresh oregano.

Serves 6

WINE PAIRING CHATEAU DE BERNE, *Côte de Provence Rose (Provence, France) 2017. The blend of Grenache and Cinsault are two of the major varietals that Provence Rosé makers use, thus giving you a classic representation of Rose to pair with this dish. The wine has a great flavor profile of strawberries and pineapple with a bit of acidity to it. There are little bits of creamy notes that come into the wine as you enjoy a glass.*

Strawberries with Marsala Zabaglione

MARSALA ZABAGLIONE
6 egg yolks
4 oz sugar

1 ¼ cup Marsala wine
2 pints fresh strawberries cut into wedges

GARNISH
Biscotti

MARSALA ZABAGLIONE

Put the egg yolks into a bowl, preferably copper, and add the sugar and Marsala. Place over a pot of boiling water and using a balloon whip, whisk the ingredients vigorously in a figure 8 motion. This allows air to enter the mix creating a much fluffier, cloudy texture. As you whip you will notice the mixture becoming thicker and rising. Once the mixture has reached its peak, it will begin to fall. This is how you know it is done.

Assembly

Place the washed, cut and dried strawberries into 6 wine glasses.
Spoon the Zabaglione over the strawberries and serve immediately. Biscotti make a nice accompaniment.

Serves 6

WINE PAIRING Vietti, Moscato d'Asti Cascinetta (Moscato d'Asti, DOCG, Italy) 2015. The Moscato d'Asti grape varietal is occasionally shunned upon as too sweet of a wine, or a cheap varietal. This is not the case when you are drinking wine from Vietti. They make some of the best Barolos in Italy. This wine has wonderful balance of acidity and fresh apricots, peaches, and ginger, perfect for a traditional Italian dessert.

ZABAGLIONE or Zabaione or even Sabayon, is a traditional dessert from Italy, made with egg yolks, sugar, and a sweet wine. This dessert is a light italian custard, whipped for a light airy consistency.

LaNONNA

MIRA AND SIMONE

Welcome to LaNonna Ristorante!
LaNonna, located in the heart of Vail Village, opened its doors on December 17, 2018. Although still in its infancy, this gorgeous restaurant has already earned a reputation as being one of "the best in Vail". Locals and tourists would agree that the food is authentic and delicious, paired perfectly with a devoted staff, passionate about creating a unique dining experience. The result of a long and extensive re-model is a space that is elegant, warm, and inviting. The kitchen is state-of-the-art with the newest and most coveted equipment.
Executive Chef/Owner Simone Riatti has revived the recipes he learned to prepare in his youth with his own "LaNonna". The menu is a reflection of that inspiration and showcases his 20 years of experience in creating the rustic, delicious cuisine of his native village in the Dolomites!

Mira Hozzova, General Manager/Owner, welcomes everyone at the front door, offering her own unique hospitality that has already generated an uber loyal following. She brings to LaNonna an extensive educational background and years of experience. Mira also possesses a genuine intuition when it comes to creating a memorable dining experience for LaNonna's beloved guests. Her passion is truly infectious!

Dining at LaNonna can be somewhat of a conundrum, as the menu is extensive and oh, so inviting. What to choose? A 24 month aged Prosciutto sliced with such precision that it literally melts in your mouth? Perhaps the PEI Mussels sauteed perfectly with garlic and fresh tomato? The real dilemma is in choosing one of the pasta dishes that LaNonna is quickly becoming famous for. Made fresh daily, using only the finest flour from Italy, guests are faced with a difficult decision. The Mushroom Ravioli in a light cream sauce with the perfect sprinkle of truffle oil? Gemelli alla Vodka e Prosciutto? Maybe the delicious fresh seafood tossed with Spaghetti and a light tomato sauce?

LaNonna is proud and excited to be a part of this cookbook, offering you an opportunity to prepare some of our deeply satisfying recipes at home for friends and family! Buon Appetito!

Growing up with my grandmother, is where all it started. The love for cooking started in that little kitchen with a banquette. Helping her cook was my playground, a warm place where all the kids and family gathered to socialize and eat grandma's delicious cooking. She was an amazing cook, but most important was to see how rewarding for her was seeing the smile on our faces.

Cooking with love is where the difference happened. Making people happy through my cooking and hospitality is the best rewards.

Finally I have my own restaurant in the best place in the world.

Live to eat, don't eat to live.

Buon appetito.

PICTURED ABOVE: Executive Chef/Owner Simone Riatti and GM/Owner Mira Hozzova

Polpo

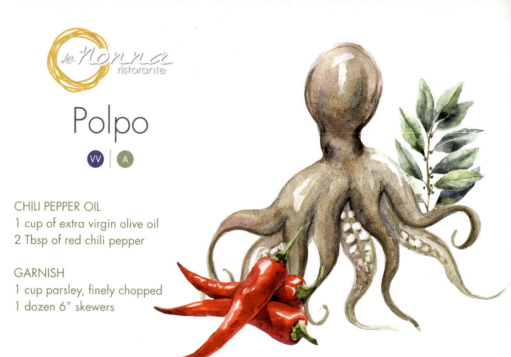

OCTOPUS
4 lbs octopus, frozen
1 carrot
1 celery stalk
1 onion
2 gloves garlic
½ cup white wine
5 white peppercorns
2 bay leaves

CHILI PEPPER OIL
1 cup of extra virgin olive oil
2 Tbsp of red chili pepper

GARNISH
1 cup parsley, finely chopped
1 dozen 6" skewers

Octopus
In a large pot boil, water and add the octopus, carrot, celery, onion, garlic, white wine, white peppercorn, and bay leaves. Cook for about 3 hours at moderate heat.
When the octopus is cooked, let it cool down until you can peel it with your hand. Cut the tentacles in 4" long stripes, then along the long axis. Then cut in half.

Chili Pepper Oil
While the octopus (Polpo) is cooking in a sauce pot, add the olive oil and the red chilli pepper and heat on the smallest flame possible for about an hour, making sure not to not burn the chilli peppers.

Grilling Octopus
When ready to eat, grill the octopus on a broiler for a few minutes each side.

Assembly
Smear a serving dish with the chilli
pepper oil, skewer octopus slices and place on top of a the chilli pepper oil olive oil and sprinkle with the parsley.
 and sprinkle with the parsley.

Garnish
Dress the octopus with chopped Italian parsley and some olive oil and put 4 pieces on each skewer.

WINE PAIRING LONG SHADOW VINEYARDS, "Poets Leap" Riesling (Columbia Valley, Washington) 2014. This wine has some delicious flavors of melon, honey, and apricot. Rieslings are separated into a few different categories. Noted as more of an "off-dry" style, this wine will have a bit more residual sugar then others. The sweetness will help balance the spice of the Chili flakes. Rieslings from this northern region in Washington are known to have great acid because of the climate being a bit cooler. Sometimes the wineries will pick the grapes a little later to allow for the grapes to ripen a bit more. Thus giving it a more off-dry style.

Gemelli alla vodka

PASTA
1 lb gemelli pasta or penne

A LA VODKA SAUCE
6 oz prosciutto, chopped
¼ cup shallots, fine chopped
2 cups heavy cream
½ cup Chef Simone's tomato sauce
¼ cup vodka
2 Tbsp Italian parsley, chopped
1 cup Parmesan cheese
canola oil

CHEF SIMONE'S TOMATO SAUCE
½ cup extra virgin olive oil
1 celery stalk, diced
1 small carrot; peeled, diced
1 small white onion, diced
1 garlic clove, crushed
2 lbs fresh Roma tomatoes, seeds removed or match weight with a can of whole plum tomatoes.

Pasta
In a large pot, boil 5 quarts of water, salted to taste. When boiling, add the gemelli or penne pasta to cook.

A la Vodka Sauce
Finely chop the shallots. In a sauce pan, add canola oil to sauté the shallots.
Add the chopped prosciutto, pour in the vodka and carefully light the mixture on fire until the alcohol is burned off. At the end, add the tomato sauce and the cream. Let the sauce reduce for a few minutes. When the pasta is cooked al dente, add it to the sauce and sauté.
Finish with a sprinkle of parsley, and you can also add some grated Parmesan.

Chef Simone's Tomato Sauce
Dice the celery, carrot and onion. In a sauce pan, add the olive oil, diced vegetables and crushed garlic, then braise them very gently. Add the diced tomatoes and sea salt to taste and bring to a boil. Lower the heat to simmer and cook for about 1 hour. There are many tomato sauce recipes for different applications, but this is the one I prefer to use at LaNonna.

WINE PAIRING ANTINORI, PIAN DELLE VIGNE, Brunello di Montalcino (Tuscany, Italy) 2013. I absolutely love this wine. With a rounder style and great red fruits as well as some acid, this wine will pair perfectly with the creamy alla vodka sauce.

ANTINORI is one of the most well known wine makers in Italy. They have wineries spread throughout Tuscany. This particular bottling is 100% Sangiovese and aged for 5 years before it is released.

Lamb Chops Agnello Ai Fichi

LAMB CHOP
(1) 7 bone rack of lamb,
 cut into 3 oz portions
1 garlic clove, chopped
1 sprig rosemary, chopped
1 sprig thyme, chopped
1 sprig sage, chopped

AGNELLO AI FICHI
2 Tbsp olive oil
2 Tbsp butter
½ cup of chopped shallots
2 cups of Port wine
1 cup dry figs, chopped
1 Tbsp fresh thyme, chopped
8 cups veal stock for demi-glace,
 (can be store bought)

Lamb Chops
The lamb chops are cut to about 3 oz each from a 7 bone rack. Marinate over night with garlic and finely chopped fresh rosemary, thyme and sage in equal part.
Grilled on a broiler or barbecue medium rare.

Demi-Glace
Feel free to use store bought as it is time consuming to make your. If you choose to make your own – in sauce pot, over medium high heat, add two cups of wine and reduce to 1 tablespoon of liquid. Add 8 cups veal stock or meat stock and reduce by ⅔. Season with salt and pepper. Strain.

Agnello Ai Fichi
In a sauce pan add olive oil and butter and sauté the shallots. Add the port wine and let it reduce in half. Add the chopped figs, thyme and demi-glace, let the mix reduce further to half again, then season with salt to taste.
This a great sauce for grilled lamb chops.

WINE PAIRING MORLET FAMILY VINEYARDS, *Coeur de Vallée, Cabernet Sauvignon (Napa Valley, California) 2014. One of my favorite wines from Napa. If you like Peter Michael but don't want to pay the top price this is your best choice. Mainly because Luc Morlet, the wine maker, used to make all of the wine at Peter Michael. If you want a true experience of the perfect pairing with this dish, this would be the one. With oak, dark fruit, and some great tannin structure. This truly is Napa Valley at its finest.*

Polenta and Broccolini

POLENTA
8 cups coarse polenta flour
2 cups water
2 bay leaves
⅓ cup Parmesan cheese, grated
⅓ cup Gorgonzola, crumbles
salt, to taste
⅓ cup Fontina cheese, grated

BROCCOLINI
2 lbs of broccolini cut off the first 2 inches as done with asparagus
½ cup julienne shallots
2 cloves garlic, sliced in half
4 Tbsp olive oil
salt and black pepper

Polenta
In a large pot add water, salt and bay leaves, and bring to boil. Slowly add the polenta, and whisk for about 3-4 minutes, then simmer for about 1½ hours at low heat, stirring with a wooden spoon from bottom to top. In a small bowl, combine the Parmesan, Gorgonzola and Fontina cheeses. Once polenta is plated, sprinkle the mixed cheeses on top to serve.

Broccolini
In a large pot heat water and a touch of salt, blanch the broccolini, strain them and cool them off in ice and water.
Sauté the shallots and the sliced garlic (do not crush the garlic, just slice in half) in the olive oil together. Add the broccolini and then season with salt and pepper to taste. Be careful not to burn the shallots and garlic.

Assembly
Place the polenta on the plate. Top with Lamb Chops Agnello Ai Fichi, or any prefered meat dish you wish. Add a side of broccolini to each plate.

Chefs
My grandmother's polenta was the best because she used a copper pot and cooked it slowly for few hours.

WINE PAIRING ISOLE E OLENA, Chianti Classico (Tuscany, Italy) 2015. Wild berries and aromatic herbs adds a nice flavor profile to the Polenta. This Sangiovese Blend gives it that body as well as the spice content. Isole e Olena is a wine you can find on many wine lists throughout the world. The wonderful spice and dried floral qualities allow for more layers to be added to this dish.

CHEF'S NOTE My grandmother's polenta was the best because she used a copper pot and cooked it slowly for few hours.

Torta di Ricotta

CRUST
6 egg yolks
2 whole eggs
18 oz cold butter
36 oz type 00 flour
10 oz cane sugar
1 lemon zest
a hint of salt

FILLING
26 oz of Impastata firm ricotta cheese
6 oz of Mascarpone cheese
6 egg yokes
6 egg white
½ oz type 00 flour
9 oz sugar
½ cup raisins soaked in triple sec
1 Tbsp of baking powder

BERRY SAUCE
4 cups of fresh or frozen mix berries
   (raspberry, blueberry, blackberry)
1 lemon, juiced
¼ cup raw sugar
2 Tbsp of Grand Marnier
½ cup of water

Pre-heat the oven to 380 degrees.

Crust
In a large bowl, combine the egg yolks, whole eggs, butter, flour, sugar, lemon zest, and salt. Mix by hand until blended and stays together. Cover the bottom of a 10 inch nonstick, round cake mold with the crust batter and cook it at 380 degrees for 10 minutes.

Filling
In a small bowl, separate the 6 egg whites and aside for later. Then in another bowl, mix the Impastata ricotta cheese, Mascarpne cheese, egg yokes, flour, sugar, raisins and baking powder. Set aside.

Whip the egg whites and fold into the filling mixture.
Once the crust is done, reduce the oven temperature to 350 degrees.

Pour the filling inside the cake mold, on top of the crust and bake it for half an hour at 350 degrees and then for an additional half hour at 285 degrees.

Berry Sauce for Torta di Ricotta
In a large sauce pan, combine ½ cup of water, the raspberries, blueberries and blackberries mix, lemon juice, sugar and Grand Marnier. Cook the mixture slowly until the sauce sticks to a spoon without running. Strain the sauce in a fine mesh to take any seeds away.

Assembly (Chef's Reccomendations)
Plate sliced Torta di Ricotta and enjoy cold with some whipped fresh heavy cream.
"This sauce is good for many delicious desserts. My favorite is vanilla gelato topped with warm berry sauce.
Torta di Ricotta can also be topped with your favorite chocolate sauce.

WINE PAIRING GASTON CHIQUET, Tradition (Champagne, France) NV. Gaston Chiquet is part of a very special selection of Houses in Champagne that make a Special Club Champagne. Made up of all three champagne grapes (Chardonnay, Pinot Noir, Pinot Meunier), creating a delicious brioche flavor with some walnut toasty notes. The pear and peach flavors also go well with the berry mixture on the top of the Torta. This Champagne with give this dish a hint of a spice cake quality on the finish.

LA TOUR

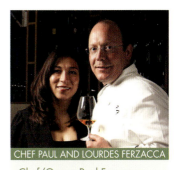

CHEF PAUL AND LOURDES FERZACCA

Welcome to La Tour Restaurant in the heart of Vail, Colorado, owned and operated by Chef Paul and Lourdes Ferzacca for the last 20 years. The Ferzaccas and their management and staff are committed to providing you the best dining experience in Vail. Honored at James Beard House, awarded Wine Spectators "Best of Award of Excellence", a Food rating of 'extraordinary' in Zagat, and Winner of Trip Advisor's Certificate of Excellence, La Tour has become one of the most acclaimed restaurants in Vail

La Tour Restaurant is a warm, cozy and very hospitality driven French~American restaurant in the Vail Village. Known for consistency, friendly professional service, excellent wines and hand crafted cocktails, La Tour is simply a must when dining in Vail. It's located directly across from the west-end of the Vail Village parking structure.

Chef Paul and Lourdes Ferzacca invite you to enjoy the finest contemporary French~American Cuisine in the Vail Valley. The La Tour team strives to have an unsurpassed standard of quality, consistency and friendly hospitality.

Chef Paul also finds time to serve on the executive committee for the Taste of Vail, the internationally acclaimed food and wine festival held in Vail each April.

La Tour offers one of the best wine lists in the state of Colorado, featuring wines from all over the world. The friendly professional wait staff will see to your every need. Reservations are recommended.

Chef/Owner Paul Ferzacca is the force behind the La Tour experience. Dedicated to developing the best restaurant in Vail, he is passionate about creating lasting memories through his carefully crafted dishes. Chef Paul has been named as "Distinguished Visiting Chef" at Johnson and Wales University in Denver, the first Colorado chef to receive this honor. Other Honors include being the feature chef at the Chesapeake Bay Wine Festival, and receiving an honorary doctorate from the Art Institute of Denver. Paul has also been a Mentor Chef for the Battle Mountain High School Pro Start restaurant management and cooking program – helping them win the state title seven out of the nine years he mentored. Taking first place in the National competition, second place twice, fourth place once and fifth place once, his students have earned over $3.5 million in scholarships as a result of his guidance.

Steak Tartare, Baby Arugula, Quail Eggs and Sauce Ravigote

SAUCE RAVIGOTE
1 shallot, brunoise
2 garlic cloves, minced
1 Tbsp whole grain mustard
2 Tbsp capers, whole
2 Tbsp cornichons, chopped fine
1 Tbsp honey
2 Tbsp champagne vinegar
6 Tbsp extra virgin olive oil
1 Tbsp kosher salt, to taste
1 Tbsp ground white pepper, to taste

GARNISH
arugula
quail eggs
long baguette croutons

TARTARE
1 lb raw Filet Mignon, hand chopped very fine, not ground
1 tsp cornichons, chopped fine
1 tsp capers, chopped fine
1 tsp shallots, cut brunoise, 1/8 x 1/8 inch
1 tsp whole grain mustard
1 tsp fresh chives, finely chopped
4 drops Tabasco® sauce
4 dashes Worcestershire sauce
2 egg yolks, raw
kosher salt, to taste
ground black pepper, to taste

Prepare the ravigote and garnishes first so the steak does not oxidize.

Sauce Ravigote
Pre-heat oven to 350 degrees.
In a mixing bowl, combine the shallot, garlic, mustard, capers, cornichons, honey and vinegar. Slowly in a steady stream add olive oil. Season with salt and ground white pepper.

Garnish
Boil your quail eggs for approximately 6 minutes until hard cooked. Peel and cut in half.
Slice baguette on bias as thin as you can, to make long croutons. Bake the sliced baguette in oven for approximately 6 minutes until golden brown.

Tartare
Hand-chop the filet mignon to a very fine consistency, but not ground. In a stainless steel bowl, mix together with the chopped filet the chopped cornichons, capers, shallots, mustard, chives, Tabasco®, Worcestershire®, egg yolk and season to taste with salt and ground black pepper.

Assembly
Plate steak tartare in ring mold, and place three croutons sticking up in tartare.
Dress arugula with a little sauce ravigote, and lightly arrange in middle of croutons.
Drizzle sauce around steak tartare and garnish with quail eggs.

WINE PAIRING MARCEL LAPIERRE, Julienas (Beaujolais, Burgundy, France) 2017. Marcel LaPierre is one of the top producers in Beujolais. One of the main grape varietals in Beaujolais is Gamay. This grape is similar to Pinot Noir in style yet a little lighter skinned. It makes for the perfect pairing to a steak tartare with its mixture of lighter red fruit such as strawberries and red cherries. You will find a hint of earthiness mixed in throughout the glass. The best part of the 2016 vintage is that it is bit smoother on the palate than the previous or following vintages. This will help cut through some of the heat for the tartare and add some nice fruit flavors. Although a red wine, it is recommended to be chilled before enjoying as it helps give it a lighter mouth-feel.

Truffled French Onion Soup with Braised Short Rib

SHORT RIBS
1 lb beef short ribs
3 oz clarified butter
1 cups Madeira wine
1 quart veal demi glace (can be store bought)
2 quarts beef stock
1 tsp kosher salt
1 tsp black pepper, ground
1 tsp white pepper, ground
1 sachet – fresh thyme, parsley,
   bay leaf, peppercorns.

ONIONS
3 oz clarified butter
2 cups Madeira wine
4 yellow onions, cut fine julienne
8 garlic cloves, sliced thin

SACHET
cheese cloth
butchers twine
fresh thyme sprigs
fresh parsley stems,

1 bay leaf
1 tsp black peppercorns

GARNISH
¼" sliced baguette 2-3 each per bowl
2-3 slices Gruyere cheese, to cover bowl
4 oz truffle cheese, grated
2 oz parmigiano-reggiano cheese, grated
1 Tbsp fresh chives

Short Ribs
Allow short ribs to come to room temperature.
Season short ribs with salt and ground black pepper.
Place a large heavy bottom stock pot on a high burner and allow to become very hot.
Add 3 ounces of clarified butter and sear short ribs until a dark golden brown on all sides.
Deglaze pan with 1 cup of Madeira wine to rehydrate meat fonds (the caramelized thickened juice) on the bottom of the pan.
Add half a quart of veal demi-glace and one quart of beef stock and bring to a simmer with sachet.
Make sure short ribs are at a low simmer and cover pan to braise short ribs until tender, approximately 2-3 hours.

Veal Demi-Glace
Store bought or you can make your own.
For home made – in a sauce pot, over medium high heat, reduce up to 2 cups of red wine down to 1 tablespoon of liquid. Add a veal or meat stock and reduce by $2/3$. Strain then season with salt and pepper.

Sachet
Place the fresh thyme sprigs, parsley stems, bay leaf and black peppercorns in the center of a square of cheesecloth.
Gather up the corners of the cheesecloth and tie off in a bundle leaving long leftover string on both ends to tie to the handler of the pot for easy extraction when done. Make sure to cut off any long ends after tying to pot to avoid a fire hazard. *Continues on page 75*

WINE PAIRING CHATEAU BLASON D'ISSAN (Margaux, Bordeaux, France) 2010. A fine aged Bordeaux is just the ticket for a Truffled French Onion Soup. When aged, a Bordeaux starts to get more "tertiary" flavors such as truffles, mushrooms, dirt, etc. This will accentuate the flavors of the truffles that are added into the soup. Chateau Blason is located on the left bank of Bordeaux. Predominately a Cabernet Sauvignon Blend with a bit of Merlot and Petit Verdot mixed in to help blend everything together, this wine has been served by the glass at some of the best restaurants throughout the world. The 2010 vintage was a bit of a hotter vintage. This vintage will release delicious dark fruit flavors to be an asset to the Short Ribs.

SACHET *is a cheese cloth filled with thyme sprigs, parsley stems, a bay leaf, and black peppercorns, then tied with twine.*

Field Green Salad with Toasted Goat Cheese Dried Cranberry, Pine Nuts, and Whole Grain Mustard Vinaigrette

SALAD
4 oz mixed greens
1 head Belgium endive, 8 large leaves
8 Pearjolais tomatoes (or any substitute)
4 tsp dried cranberries
4 tsp pine nuts
1 tsp chervil
1 tsp parsley
1 tsp tarragon
1 tsp chives

Kosher salt to taste
white pepper, ground to taste

TOASTED GOAT CHEESE
4 oz goat cheese
1 cup all purpose flour
1 whole egg
1 Tbsp milk
1 cup breadcrumbs
2 oz pure olive oil

WHOLE GRAIN MUSTARD VINAIGRETTE
1 tsp whole grain mustard
1 tsp honey
1 shallot
1 garlic clove
1 Tbsp Champagne vinegar
3 Tbsp extra virgin olive oil
½ tsp kosher salt
¼ tsp white pepper, ground

Toasted Goat Cheese
Slice the cheese into 4 one-ounce pieces.
Place in freezer until very hard.
Prepare breading station; mix egg and milk in a bowl to create an egg wash. Place flour in a separate bowl and breadcrumbs in an additional bowl.
Once cheese is hard, dredge in flour then egg wash then breadcrumbs. Place back in freezer. You can prepare the cheese up to three days in advance.
When ready to toast the cheese, remove from the freezer and sauté over high heat with pure olive oil just enough to toast the bread crumbs, about 30 seconds each side. Remove from pan and place on paper towel. You can now refrigerate the cheese until ready to serve salad. Before serving, reheat the toasted cheese in oven at 350 degrees until just heated through, about 5 minutes.

The Vinaigrette
In small stainless steel bowl mince the shallot and garlic and combine with the mustard, honey, vinegar, salt and white pepper. Slowly add the extra virgin olive oil, in a small stream, while whisking to completely emulsify the vinaigrette. Once all of the oil is incorporated, taste the vinaigrette to check the seasoning. Add more salt or pepper, if needed.

The salad
Toast the pine nuts in a 350 degrees oven for 4 minutes or until golden brown. Once toasted let cool completely. *Continues on page 75*

WINE PAIRING REGIS MINET, Pouilly Fumé (Pouilly-Fume, Loire, France) 2016. A Pouilly Fume is just the wine for this dish. Goat Cheese, a bit richer, creamier, style of cheese. Pouilly Fume, which is made from Sauvignon Blanc has a flinty, smokey texture (Fumé in French means "smokey"). This wine will have vibrant acid as well as some tropical flavors with touches of mango, guava, and pear and a pleasant flavor of minerality that keeps you wanting more.

Dover Sole Meunière with Haricots Vert, Baby Creamer Potatoes with Lemon Brown Butter Sauce

DOVER SOLE
4 Dover Sole, filets
4 oz clarified butter or canola oil
1 cup all purpose flour

CREAMER POTATOES
8 baby creamer potatoes,
   (you can substitute red bliss)

HARICOTS VERT and TOMATOES
4 oz haricots vert,
   (or you can substitute green beans)
salt (to heavily salt water)
2 Roma tomatoes

LEMON BROWN BUTTER SAUCE
2 fresh lemons
4 oz heavy cream

4 oz whole butter non-salted
kosher salt to taste
white pepper, ground to taste

GARNISH
2 Roma tomatoes
3 tsp chives
2 fresh lemon, cut into wedges

Creamer Potatoes
Place potatoes in a small pot and cover with cold water. Add 2 teaspoons of salt and bring to a boil. Once boiling, turn down to a simmer and let cook until potatoes are fork tender. Remove from water and let cool on a sheet pan. Once cool, refrigerate until needed. This procedure can be done one day in advance.

Haricots Vert and Tomatoes
In another 2 quart pot, fill with water and bring to a boil. While that is coming to a boil, with small paring knife, remove the stems from the Roma tomatoes and score an X on the other end of tomato to prepare them for blanching to remove the skin and seeds. Also, remove the ends of the haricots vert, and reserve for blanching.
Set up an ice bath with plenty of ice and cold water to refresh the tomatoes and haricots vert once blanched.
Once the water is at a rolling boil, blanch the Roma tomatoes

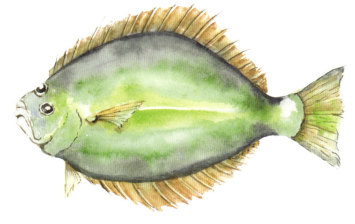

for about 15 seconds to just blister the skin and refresh in the ice bath. Remove from ice bath, let drain, keep ice bath to refresh haricots vert.
Now season the boiling water with enough salt to make it taste like the ocean. This will retain the color *Continues on page 76*

WINE PAIRING GUY ROBIN, 1er Cru, Montee de Tonnerre (Burgundy, France) 2016. Montee de Tonnerre is a well-known vineyard in the village of Chablis, North of Burgundy proper, is still part of Burgundy so the main white grape varietal is Chardonnay. With the limestone and chalky soils in the region, Chablis is known to have excellent minerality, giving the wine a vibrant and racy style. This should cut through the creaminess of the Lemon Brown butter sauce quite nicely. With lemony notes along with a bit of wet stone will allow the Lemon to come through from the sauce.

Crème Brûlée Flambé with Grand Marnier Macerated Berries

CRÈME BRÛLÉE
16 oz heavy cream
3 oz sugar
1 vanilla bean whole fresh
3 egg yolks
1 whole egg

MACERATED BERRIES
8 strawberries 8 each
¼ pint raspberries
¼ pint blackberries
¼ pint blueberries
2 oz Grand Marnier

TOPPING / BRULÉE THE CUSTARD
½ cup granulated sugar
1 sifter 1 ea
1 propane torch
1 oz 151 Bacardi Rum

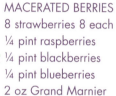

Pre-heat oven to 325 degrees.

Crème Brûlée

Split vanilla bean in half and scrape out all beans inside. Place beans and skin inside a 2-quart pot. Add the cream and sugar. Scald the cream by bringing the liquid to a boil. Keeping a careful eye on the pot, stir occasionally, so as not to let the cream boil over. While the cream is coming to a boil; crack your eggs and separate into a stainless steel bowls. Whisk eggs yolks with the one egg until combined.

Once cream is scalded, temper the cream into the eggs by very slowly adding the cream to the eggs and constantly stirring. Strain the crème brûlèe batter through a fine chinois and ladle about 6 ounces into each of 4 crème brûlèe dishes.

Place the dish on a flat sheet pan and in a preheated oven. Add water until it reaches half way up crème brulee dish. Bake crème brûlèe for about 45 minutes or until the custard is firm. Remove from oven and let cool completely. Place in the refrigerator until needed for plating (can be made up to three days in advance).

Grand Marnier Macerated Berries

Slice strawberries into quarters and place in small stainless steel bowl then add the blackberries, blueberries and raspberries to the strawberries. Add the Grand Marnier and let macerate about 30 minutes in refrigerator.

When ready to plate, remove crème brûlée from refrigerator and sift sugar on top of custard until a small amount creates a white coating. Brûlèe with propane torch until the entire top is golden brown.

Assembly

Garnish the top of the crème brûlée with the macerated berries. Place a half of a capful of 151 Bacardi Rum on top of crème brûlée and ignite with a lighter.

Make sure your guests lets the alcohol burn off. Do not blow out or eat while on fire.

Serves 4.

WINE PAIRING DOW'S 20 Year Tawny Port (Upper Douro Valley, Portugal). A staple in most restaurants. I personally love a good 20, or 40 year tawny port with Creme Brûlée. Port is a fermented red wine that has aromas and flavors of chocolate, dark berries, and has a sweet finish. Dow's is one of the top producers of Porto in the region and has been making Porto for over two centuries.

MACERATE rather than to marinate which is using liquid such as oil or water and spices to macerate refers to soaking fruit in your favorite alcohol which will soften it. Using sugared combined with Grand Marnier, the berries release their own juices, end result a wonderful a sweet liquid.

Field Green Salad with Toasted Goat Cheese, Dried Cranberry, Pine Nuts and Whole Grain Mustard Vinaigrette Cream (cont'd)

Field Green Salad with Toasted Goat Cheese con't from page 72

Prepare fine herbs: Rough chop all herbs (chervil, parsley, chives and tarragon), mix together and reserve to season salad. Make sure greens are clean. If not, wash in cold water in a large bowl. Dry the greens very well.

Cut about 1" off the bottom of the Belgium endive and peel off 8 each leaves to garnish the salad.
Cut the Pearjolais tomatoes in half and reserve to garnish salad. Once you are ready to serve salad to your guest, heat up goat cheese in oven at 350 degrees for about 5 minutes.
In a large bowl, combine mixed greens, Belgium endive, fine herbs, kosher salt, ground white pepper and about 2 to 3 tablespoons of vinaigrette. Toss gently to combine. Plate endive first on plate at 10 and 2 o'clock, place salad in middle of plate, place tomatoes at 5 and 7 o'clock and place warm goat cheese leaning up against salad at 6 o'clock.

Truffled French Onion Soup with Braised Short Rib (cont'd)

Truffled French Onion Soup con't from page 74

Onions
While short ribs are braising, add another heavy bottom pan to a high burner and allow to become very hot.
Add 3 ounces of clarified butter and cook onions until very well caramelized, scraping bottom of pan often so they do not burn. Remember the onions must be well caramelized.
Add garlic and sweat 2 minutes.
Deglaze with remaining 1 cup Madeira wine and remaining 1 quart of beef stock.
Bring to a simmer and combine with short ribs for the last hour or so of braising time of short ribs.
When short ribs are tender, remove and shred or cut into small pieces to be able to fit on a soup spoon and place back in soup. Add fresh thyme, parsley and season with salt and ground white pepper.

Croutons
Pre-heat oven to 350 degrees.
Slice baguette ¼" thin, place on sheet pan, brush with clarified butter and season with salt and ground white pepper. Bake croutons in 350 degrees oven until golden brown and crispy. About 6 minutes.

Assembly
Turn oven to Broil.
Ladle soup in ceramic heat proof bowls, place 2-3 croutons in soup, cover croutons and sides of bowl with Gruyere cheese, sprinkle truffle cheese on, and grated Parmesan.
Place bowls under broiler and gratinate cheese to completely cover bowls.
Remove soup from broiler and garnish with fresh chopped chives.

Yields half gallon.

Dover Sole Meunière with Haricots Vert, Baby Creamer Potatoes

Dover Sole Meunière, con't from page 73 of the beans when cooking. Note: green vegetables release acid into the water and the evaporation, which will discolor the vegetables. To counteract the acid, an alkaline must be added to the water. Salt is an excellent alkaline. Also, do not cover the pot or the acid released in the evaporation will be dispersed back into the water.

Once the water is back at a rolling boil and seasoned with salt, blanch the haricots vert for about 5 minutes or until al dente. The starches should be jelled completely when cooking any bean, to aid in the digestion process. Remove beans and refresh in ice bath. Once chilled again, remove from water, let drain and reserve for plating. This step can be done one day in advance.

Lemon Brown Butter Sauce

Combine the heavy cream and butter in a 2 quart sauce pan, bring to a boil and reduce to simmer. Note: When bringing to boil stir occasionally and watch carefully so as the cream does not boil over. Once reduced to a simmer stir occasionally, allow to cook until the cream and butter breaks.

Once the cream and butter breaks you must stir constantly to toast the milk solids until golden brown. This will happen quickly; be careful not to burn the milk solids.

Once milk solids are golden brown, remove from pan and allow cooling in a different container.

Once cooled, but still liquid, puree in blender to break up milk solids. You can make the brown butter one week in advance and just reheat in a water bath when needed.

Garnish

Remove skin from tomatoes and cut into quarters lengthwise, remove seeds then dice the tomato fillets into ¼" pieces. Reserve in small dish for garnishing plates.

Prepare the chives: Slice into ⅛ inch pieces, reserve in small dish for garnishing plate.

Dover Sole

Remove skin from both sides of the fish and fillet the meat to yield 4 fillets from each fish. This can be done one day in advance.

Season fish with salt and ground white pepper, dredge in flour and sauté in clarified butter or canola oil until golden brown.

Assembly

Place brown butter sauce in a hot water bath in double boiler and bring back up in temperature.

Have a small pot of water on stove to reheat potatoes and haricots vert. Before cooking fish, place potatoes and haricots vert in water and reheat. Once hot remove and season with salt and ground white pepper.

Once fish is done, remove and place on plate with potatoes, haricots vert. Sauce the fish, potatoes and haricots vert with brown butter sauce, garnish plate with diced tomatoes, chives and squeeze fresh lemon juice over everything.

Serves 4.

THE LEFT BANK

JEAN-MICHEL CHELAIN

Left Bank Restaurant serves traditional French cuisine with a modern twist in the heart of Vail Village. Using the freshest ingredients of the finest quality, chef Jean-Michel Chelain prepares every dish from scratch. Think classics like pepper steak and Bouillabaisse de Crustacés au Fenouil. Each item is carefully prepared and beautifully presented to offer a culinary experience unlike any other. We hope to have the pleasure of serving you not just to eat, but to dine.

In 2006, Jean-Michel Chelain became the owner of Left Bank, a restaurant specializing in French cuisine, which he says "is sometimes misunderstood". "When people think of French food, they think of it as being very heavy, which is not necessarily the case. Of course, we have foie gras and bisque, but my philosophy is that food should be made with the least amount of ingredients. It should be made with the freshest ingredients, whole ingredients, all products that the body can break down.

Though traditionally trained, and a purist when it comes to how he prepares classic French fare, Chef Jean-Michel describes his cooking as not very traditional at all. His menu supports this claim. Dishes such as a Fresh Boneless Trout sauteed with olive oil, capers, caper berries, tomatoes and fine herbs or his fresh salmon baked with olive oil, garlic, tomatoes and fresh herbs share billing with such traditional dishes as Bouillabaisse de Crustaces au Fenuill, and a well known dessert favorite, chocolate souffle.

Keep in mind that when visiting Left Bank in Vail Colorado, Chef Chelain augments his set menu, which he updates seasonally and allows his creativity and artistry to flourish.

It's important to Chef Chelain to establish a standard and continue to meet it. He says that they can serve between 150 and 180 patrons in an evening and strives to maintain a quality of cuisine, and services, maintaining an outstanding experience for all.

Growing up in the French Alps, Chef Chelain began pursuing his culinary muse at a tender age. Chef Chelain recalls, "when I was about nine years-old I began baking cakes. In the French school system, we had Wednesdays off and all I ever wanted to do on Wednesdays was to bake cakes."

Chef Chelain began his two-year apprenticeship at age sixteen, and at age eighteen he began working in kitchens in Cannes and on the Cote d'Azur before coming to the United States in 1996. Once in the U.S., Chef Chelain went to work in Carmel, California at Stone Pine, a 4-star rated Relais Chateau, before moving on to Vail.

Chef Chelain has a personal affinity for the apprenticeship method of learning the culinary arts. It served him well, and now he's the master training his own professionals.

Waygu Tartar

WAYGU TARTAR STEAK
18 oz of Waygu tenderloin trimmed, no fat
1 oz capers
1 oz shallots
1 oz Cornichon pickles
parsley
anchovies, to taste

cayenne pepper to taste
drizzle of Worcestershire™
drizzle of olive oil
salt, to taste
pepper, to taste
2 egg yolks

OPTIONAL
½ oz of ketchup
½ oz of Dijon mustard

GARNISH
grilled or toasted bread

Waygu Tartar

Cut the beef tenderloin in small cubes and set aside in a large bowl. Keep cubed beef cold (in a large bowl over an ice bath or set aside in the freezer) while preparing the other ingredients. In a separate bowl, mix together the finely chopped capers, shallots, cornichon pickles, parsley, and anchovies to taste. Add cayenne pepper to taste, a drizzle of Worcestershire sauce and olive oil. Mix well. Once completely chopped, add the mixture to the diced beef.
Lightly beat egg yolks, add to diced beef and mix well.
Season with salt and pepper to taste.
You can also add ½ an ounce of ketchup and/or Dijon mustard.
Serve on grilled or toasted bread.

Serves 6

Preparation of Raw Meat

Classic Waygu Tartare is served raw. When handling raw meat, use work surfaces and utensils that are very clean. To ensure the meat remains chilled during preparation (below 45 degrees), place it in the freezer prior to dicing for about 20 minutes until it is firm but not frozen.

WINE PAIRING MOULIN-A-VENT DES HOSPICES (Beaujolais, Burgundy, France) 2015. A Steak Tartare, particularly a Waygu version, needs to have the perfect pairing. A Beaujolais is exactly the right choice. Moulin-a-Vent is a producer that has a different style. They do 20% whole cluster fermentation (meaning, they add some of the stems of the grapes into the fermentation tanks, giving it more tannin structure). After aging it for 18 months in oak and steel you get a brilliant aroma of deep red fruits, spice, and floral notes. A great pairing for the tartare, not too light, yet not too heavy, just perfect.

WAYGU literally means Japanese beef. It's exquisite flavor, texture, and tenderness make this highly-marbled beef a coveted favorite among Chefs in Asia, across the U.S., and throughout the world. Selective breeding and rigorous standards explain why Waygu is considered as the best in the world. Certified Kobe beef is a well-known regional variety of Waygu produced in the Hyoso perfecture in Japan. After a ban on Japanese beef in the 2000's ended, Australia, the United Kingdom, and the U.S. began to produce high-quality Waygu, making this delicious cut more accessible.

Lobster Roll

LOBSTER ROLL
2 live lobsters, 1¼-1½ lbs,

BOUILLON
3 qts of water
1 small onion, chopped
1 small carrot, chopped
1 celery stalk
3 bay leaves
rock salt
cracked pepper

MAYONNAISE
2 yolks
1 tsp spoon Dijon mustard
1 cup of vegetable oil
2 tsp Champagne vinegar
1 pinch salt and pepper

LOBSTER SALAD
2 oz celery
2 oz white fennel
2 oz yellow onions
½ fresh lemon juice
pinch cayenne pepper
salt and pepper, to taste
bibb lettuce
mayonnaise

POTATO BREAD
2 large eggs
⅓ cup sugar
2 tsp salt
6 Tbsp butter, softened
1 cup of mashed potato (1 lrg potato)
2 tsp dry yeast
¾ cup water or milk (warm)
4¼ cup baking flour

Lobster Bouillon
Bring 3 quarts of water to a boil. Add the chopped onion, chopped carrot, celery branch, 3 bay leaves, rock salt and cracked pepper. Submerge the lobster and cook to a simmer for 8 minutes. Next, cool the lobster in a cold water bath and break down the shell. Removed the tail meat and cut in large pieces for the lobster salad.

Mayonnaise
In a blender mix together the egg yolks and Dijon mustard. Slowly add the vegetable oil and then finish by adding the champagne vinegar and salt and pepper.

Lobster Salad
In a medium bowl, mix together the lobster pieces, celery, fennel, and onion. Add the home made mayonnaise, lemon juice, cayenne pepper and, salt and pepper to taste.

Potato Bread
Mix together – by hand or mixer, the 2 large eggs, sugar, salt, softened butter, mashed potato, dry yeast, water or milk (warm), and baking flour.
Place the dough in a mixing bowl, cover the bowl with plastic wrap, and let the dough rise until it's doubled in bulk, about 90 minutes. Divide it into 10 large balls. Round each ball into a smooth roll.
Place the rolls in a lightly greased pan. Cover the pan with lightly greased plastic wrap, and let them rise for 1½ to 2 hours until they're quite puffy. Towards the end of the rising time, preheat the oven to 350 degrees.
Bake the rolls for 20 to 25 minutes, until they're golden brown and feel set. Remove from the oven, and remove from pan onto a rack.

Cut your potato bread rolls in half and top lettuce on 1 side then top with the lobster salad and finish with the other side of the bun.

WINE PAIRING WILLIAM FÈVRE, Les Champs Royaux (Chablis, Burgundy, France) 2017. Lobster, a rich seafood, is best paired with a crisper style white wine. Chablis is known to have a bit more minerality in it than other French whites. This wine will give off a bouquet of flowers, green apple, and wet stone and will be a perfect pairing for a lobster salad with a mayonnaise sauce. It will give the dish a more citrus flavor to accentuate the flavors of the dish as a whole.

Fresh Alaskan Halibut

HALIBUT
6 halibut, skinless, thick steaks
olive oil
salt/pepper
2 oz white wine
24 grape tomato

ASAPARAGUS
2 bundle of asparagus
¼ cup olive oil, as needed
sea salt

PESTO RECIPE
8 oz fresh basil
1 small bunch of parsley
6 small garlic glove
6 oz of olive oil
3 oz of grated parmesan cheese

Halibut
Pan sear the halibut in a hot pan with olive oil for 1 minute, flip it over, add the white wine and season with salt and pepper. Cut the grape tomatoes in half and add them all to the pan. Put the pan in the oven to bake for 5 minute at 400 degrees.

Cut and wash the asparagus and toss them in olive oil adding some sea salt and pepper. Put the asparagus on a hot grill and roll them constantly to cook them evenly.

Pesto
In a blender, put half of the olive oil first, then add the peeled garlic and basil leaf with the parsley. Start blending, adding little by little the rest of the olive oil and the parmesan cheese and finish with salt and pepper then set aside.

Assembly
Remove the fish from the pan and place the halibut steaks on the grilled asparagus.
Add the pesto to the white wine and tomato reduction, bring to a boil and serve it over the fish.

Serves 6

WINE PAIRING DOMAINE BOUCHARD Pouilly Fuissé (Burgundy, France) 2016. Bouchard is one of the oldest Burgundy producers so you know this comes from a great house. Pouilly Fuissé is known to have a crisp and light flavor which works well with this meaty fish. With a white peach and vanilla flavor that this wine gives off it gives an elegant flavor profile combination with the pesto. The finish also leaves a wet stone and dry mineral flavor to it, this will give it a bit more fresh finish to the dish.

Elk Chop and Red Wine Sauce with Wild Mushrooms

ELK CHOPS
2.5 to 2.8 lbs all natural elk rack, french cut
salt and cracked pepper, to taste
butter
olive oil

SHALLOT and WILD MUSHROOM
2 large shallots
2 cup wild or organic mushrooms
1 cup red wine (Cabernet Sauvignon)
glace de viande, to taste

beef stock, for glace de viande
salt and pepper, to taste

French Cut Chops
Cut 1 or 2 chop per person, depending on the size of the chop. Score the lamb chops across all the rib bones on each side where the meat thins out to create a clean cut and to expose the rib bones leaving the bulk of the meat on the bone. Do this on both sides cutting the meat between the ribs as you go so you can peel off the meat from the ribs.
If preferred, have your butcher French cut your chops for you.

Elk Chops
In a hot sauté pan, heat the butter and olive oil. To sear the elk chops, place them in the heated butter and oil for 3 to 4 minutes on each side depending on the desired temperature. Place the pan to rest on a plate on the side of the stove.

Shallot and Wild Mushroom Ragout
Using the same pan, suer the thinly sliced shallots and the wild mushrooms for 1 or 2 minute. Deglaze the shallot and mushrooms with the red wine, add the glace de viande, season to taste and simmer to reduce to the right, syrupy consistency.

Glace de Viande
Use unsalted stock, especially if store-bought stock.
In a large saucepan, heat meat stock to a boil. Reduce heat to medium and simmer. Skim solids from the surface as the stock cooks. Simmer until stock is reduced to slightly more than ½. Strain over a medium pot using a mesh strainer lined with cheesecloth.
Place stock back on the stove over medium-low heat. Continue reducing until the glace is reduced by three-quarters and the consistency is thick and syrupy (it will coat the back of a spoon when finished).

Assembly
Place the elk chop in a dish and serve it with a little ragout of shallot and wild mushrooms and a drizzle of red wine reduction.

Serves 4
Bonne Appétit!

WINE PAIRING SILVER OAK Cabernet (Sonoma County, California) 2014. Known by many as one of the best cult wines in California, Silver Oak reigns above all. The chocolate and vanilla flavor allows for the more gamey flavors of this elk dish to culminate into a delicious intertwining flavor profile that pairs incredibly well.
Silver Oak has 24 months of new and old American Oak which make it a richer style Cabernet from California. If you like that richer style of wine to pair with this dish there is nothing better than this classic California Cabernet.

CHOCOLATE MOUSSE CAKE

CHOCOLATE MOUSSE CAKE
6 oz 72% Valrhona chocolate
3 egg yolks
1 whole egg (chef recommended 30 grams)
⅓ cup sugar
½ oz water
1½ cups whipped cream (soft peak)

VALRHONA CHOCOLATE GANACHE
4 oz Valrhona chocolate
3½ oz cream
1 Tbsp Grand Marnier
2 Tbsp honey

WHIPPED CREAM
heavy cream

ALMOND BISCUITS
3 egg whites
½ cup blanched almond flour
½ cup powdered sugar
2 drop vanilla extract
1 drop lemon juice
parchment paper

Chocolate Mousse Cake
In a mixing bowl, whip the 1 whole egg plus the yolks at full speed and set aside.
In a sauce pan, cook the sugar and water to a soft ball, meaning that when you drop a spoonful into a small dish of cold water the sugar will solidify and moldable into a small ball, this happens at 235 degrees. Once at boil, add the sugar water mixture slowly to the eggs mixture. Whip the combined mixture to a soft sabayon (custard consistency).

Set aside the chocolate and items listed for the Valrhona Chocolate ganache, this comes later.
Melt the 6 oz of chocolate for the best consistency you must temper the chocolate. (See page 83 for tempering chocolate). Once melted properly, add the chocolate to the egg and sugar mixture, then fold in the whipped cream. Pour mousse mixture in pan or dish of choice and cover with plastic film. Refrigerate it for 2 of hours.

Valrhona Chocolate Ganache
In a sauce pan, add the cream and bring to a boil. Mix in the honey and Grand Marnier then remove it from heat. While still hot, add the 4 oz of chocolate to the cream and let it melt. Use a whisk to blend the ganache. Set aside keeping the ganache at room temperature until ready to use.

Whipped Cream
In a mixing bowl whip the heavy cream to soft peaks and set aside, ready to fold into mousse cake.

Almond Biscuits
Preheat the oven at 350 degrees.
In a mixing bowl, whip the egg whites, lemon juice and vanilla extract to firm peaks. Slowly incorporate the powered sugar and almond flour. Once mixed, pour into a baking pan and bake for 10 minutes. The biscuit should stay soft.

Continues on page 87

WINE PAIRING CHATEAU COUTET Sauternes (Bordeaux, France) 1997. While this Chateau is greatly overshadowed by the ever so well-known Chateau d'Yquem, this Chateau makes some splendid Sauternes. Sauternes comes from a smaller appellation within Bordeaux, just to the South. The "noble rot" allows for the grapes to ripen a bit more allowing it to rot ever so slightly to give the wine more of a raisin look to it. The flavor profile gives off a flinty and rich nose. The concentrated flavors of apricot and nectarine are jumping out of the glass for this Sauternes. This glass will make an amazing pairing with a rich Chocolate Cake.

🅐 Chocolate Mousse Cake

Chocolate Mousse Cake, con't from page 86

Assembly

Remove the chocolate mousse cake from the refrigerator. Flip the pan and remove the cake onto a cake plate. Pour the tempered chocolate ganache to cover the cake. Smooth the ganache over the top and sides and return to the refrigerator for another hour to set. Top it off with the almond biscuit.

Tempered Chocolate

Tempering creates the signature appearance, texture, and taste of fine chocolates. By slowly heating and cooling melted chocolate while stirring, the cocoa butter crystallizes evenly. Use tempered chocolate before it cools and sets; re-temper if chocolate has solidified. Chocolate will stay in temper and retain the right consistency to use if kept at the correct temperature – 88-91 degrees fahrenheit for dark chocolate or 87-88 degrees fahrenheit for milk or white chocolate.

To better control temperature changes while tempering chocolate, consider doubling the amount to 1½ pounds of chocolate. Reserve the additional chocolate not used in preparing the mousse cake and ganache.

Heat a saucepan with water to just below the bottom of a double boiler or metal bowl to simmering. Place two-thirds of the chocolate in a double boiler or metal bowl and set onto the saucepan. Place a candy or digital thermometer in the chocolate, stirring frequently with a rubber spatula. Heat chocolate slowly. For dark chocolate, do not exceed 250 degrees, or 220 degrees for milk or white chocolate. Remove from heat when fully melted but keep the saucepan with simmering water on heat.

Add the remaining third of the chocolate a little at a time, stirring to melt and combine before adding more.

Once the chocolate is at 180 degrees fahrenheit, place it back over simmering water. For dark chocolate, reheat to 190-195 degrees fahrenheit. For milk and white chocolate, reheat to 185 degrees to 189 degrees. Remove the bowl from heat once you have reached the right temperature.

To test readiness, spread a small spoonful of chocolate on a piece of wax paper. Chocolate is in temper if it dries quickly with no streaks and a glossy finish. Re-temper the chocolate if it looks dull or streaky by placing it back over simmering water and reheating to the correct temperature.

VALRHONA *is an artisan quality chocolate produced in the small Rhone Valley village of Tain L'Hermitage, in France since 1922. A strict, hands-on process starting with how their cacao is grown to monitoring production by highly trained chefs has produced some of the finest chocolate in the world.*

BISTRO | WINE | TAPAS BAR

LENORA BISTRO & TAPAS BAR

Tucked just steps off Vail Village's cobblestone pedestrian corridor sits restaurant Leonora. This playfully sophisticated bistro pairs tapas-style dishes with wines from around the world. Named for Leonora Carrington, a famous Mexican surrealist painter and novelist, this hidden gem honors her legacy with edible works of art composed of fresh, organic and locally-sourced ingredients. Located inside The Sebastian – Vail, a 130 room luxury boutique hotel which is adorned with Carrington's works, a warm and inviting dining room beckons you with an impressive 350 bottle wine tower at center stage. Wine connoisseurs are met with bottles stacked to the ceiling, providing the perfect vintage to complement each robust flavor from Executive Chef Tyson Peterson's kitchen.

The menu is designed as a tapas experience, one where diners embark with shareable small plates, pintxos (similar to tapas but from the Basque area) and cheese and charcuterie before progressing to larger plates which revere alpine flavors including Colorado lamb pops, elk tartare and local steaks and more. For a traditional dish with a Vail flair, try Chef Tyson's fried chicken with barrel-aged Fresno hot sauce. Supplement your selections with caviar tins, Hovey & Harrison hearth bread or Winter truffles.

A sumptuous night out in Vail is perfected with a sweet send-off. Indulge in Pastry Chef Amaya Laws' confections paired with a fitting digestif; perhaps a decadent six-layer praline raspberry cake, seasonal cobbler, strawberry snowball or flourless chocolate cake.

We hope you enjoy the tastes of Leonora and invite you to experience the mouth-watering artistry in person.

CHEF TYSON PETERSON

Executive Chef at The Sebastian —Vail Chef Tyson was born and raised in the mountains of Utah and realized his passion for cooking in the outdoors. Hunting large game, camping, and cooking over woodfire coals where feeding approximately 50 people, proved an enjoyable challenge.

After Culinary school, Chef Tyson returned to Park City, Utah. There he developed his pedigree, most notably as Sous Chef for world class Chef Jean George at his restaurant the "J&G Grill" located slope-side at The St. Regis Hotel, Deer Valley.

At Leonora, Chef Tyson and his team create Tapas style dishes inspired by Spanish cuisine and the surrounding Rocky Mountains agriculture. Many of the menu's ingredients are sourced from local farmers and artisans including game meats and produce.

Ono Crudo with Crunchy Garlic and Yuzu

ONO CRUDO
1 lb "Saku" blocks of Hawaiian Ono
(can be substituted with any sashimi grade fish)
salt
vegetable oil

FOR THE PONZU
2 oz sweet soy sauce
2 oz light sodium soy sauce
3 oz Yuzu juice (sub- half lemon, half lime)
1 Tbsp Sriracha hot sauce
1 tsp sesame oil
salt as needed
1 oz rice vinegar for an extra acidic pop

FOR THE GARNISH
1 bottle "Ryu" or "Crunchy Garlic topping"
1 Asian yellow pear, julienned
1 bunch cilantro, chiffonade

Assemble
Place the sliced fish on a plate and dress the fish with spoonfuls of Ponzu.
Scoop small amounts of "Ryu" on each slice of fish.
Scatter pear on top of fish and sprinkle cilantro over all items.
Add more dressing as desired.

Ono Crudo
Cut fish in half or into 8 oz portions length-wise.
Season with salt and rub lightly with oil.
Sear or flash grill each side quickly (10 to 15 seconds per side). Rest and reserve in refrigerator. Do not try to cook further as this is a raw application.
Once chilled, use sharpest knife to cut finger-width slices. Reserve chilled.

Ponzu
Whisk together the sweet soy sauce, light sodium soy sauce, Yuzu juice, Sriracha hot sauce, sesame oil, salt and rice vinegar if you desire an extra acidic pop. Taste and adjust seasoning with more salt or citrus until flavor is balanced.

WINE PAIRING VINO ZORZAL, Granacha Blanc (Navarra, Spain). Great minerality and clean finish. Located in the heart of the Navarra's Ribera Baja region, Spains version of Grenache Blanc, set on hillsides bordering the Ebro Valley and Iberian Mountains. There are aromas of citrus fruit, stone fruits such as peach and apricot. This should pair perfectly with the Crudo.

PONZU Citrus and soy dressing/sauce ideal for many seafood applications.
YUZU Japanese citrus in juice form with a unique fragrance and aromatic quality.
RYU S&B brand crunchy garlic topping can be found in Asian markets.

Elk Tartare with Hazelnut and Blueberries

TARTARE
10 oz small diced elk sirloin
1 oz extra virgin olive oil
1 pinch chili flake
1 pinch salt
1 oz shallot, minced

HAZELNUT DRESSING
1 oz egg yolks (about 1)
2 oz cornichons, drained
½ oz hazelnuts, toasted
1 oz lemon juice
1 pinch salt
7 oz vegetable oil
1 oz hazelnut oil
½ pinch chili flakes
½ oz water

SOURDOUGH CRISPS
1 loaf hearth bread, sliced thin
4 oz butter, unsalted
hazelnut oil
sea salt

GARNISH (FAMILY STYLE)
2 oz your favorite granola
1 oz hazelnuts, toasted, lightly crushed
4 oz hazelnut dressing
4 oz blueberries, cut in half
sea salt

Tartare
Put the sirloin in a bowl and drizzle with the olive oil – mix well. Just before you are ready to serve, add the chili flakes, salt and minced shallot and mix well. Remember this should be the moment before you are ready to serve.

For the hazelnut dressing
Put the cornichons and hazelnuts in the blender and blend to medium fine consistency. Add the egg yolk, lemon juice, water, salt and chili flakes to the blender and process. Drizzle in the vegetable and hazelnut oils until emulsified. Reserve and chill until needed

Sourdough Crisps
Lightly butter one side of the bread and cook, butter side down in a hot pan until well-toasted and crunchy. Flip bread and cook the other side until toasted and crunchy. Drizzle lightly with hazelnut oil and sea salt

Assembly
Serve family style on 1 plate, or use a ring mold to portion individually on separate plates.
Spoon the hazelnut dressing on the plate and top the dressing with the tartare. Garnish with granola, toasted hazelnuts and blueberries. Place the sourdough crisps around the tartare then sprinkle sea salt on top of tartare as desired.
To finish, drizzle with olive oil lightly to make the tartare shine as desired.

WINE PAIRING *La Vitoriana, Mencia (Bierzo, Spain) 2015. Mencia grape has earth and berry undertones.*
Raúl Pérez makes a fantastic Mencia using Organic practices for farming techniques. Located in the Northwest area of Spain the grapes are grown on sandy clay soil giving the wine a brightness and focused mineral flavor profile. The aromas of raspberry, blueberry, and red/black currant will help accentuate those blueberry notes with the tartare.

leonora
BISTRO | WINE | TAPAS BAR

Crispy Octopus with Fingerling Potatoes and Chorizo

OCTOPUS
1 octopus, whole
7 black peppercorns
5 garlic cloves
1 bay leaf
2 lemons, cut in half
5 sprigs of thyme
cheese cloth & twine

1 ½ gal water
8 oz salt

POTATOES
2 fingerlings,
    cut into 1 inch pieces
3 oz salt
water as needed

SAUCE
4 oz garlic, minced
6 oz olive oil
½ oz Spanish paprika
4 oz cured chorizo, small dice
2 ea juice of fresh lemon
2 oz parsley chiffonade
lemon wedges for garnish

Octopus

Place the black peppercorns, garlic cloves, bay leaf, lemon halves and sprigs of thyme, into the cheese cloth and tie securely with twine, creating a sachet. Set aside.

Add most of the water to a large pot and bring to a boil (you may not need all the water). Once boiling, add the salt and the sachet and return to a rolling boil.
Holding the entire octopus by the head slowly dip the tentacles into the boiling water. Gently repeat the dip 3 times. This simple step helps the tentacles curl evenly. Once you have dipped 3 times, submerge the octopus into the water completely. Add more water to cover as needed (you may even need to place a plate on top of the octopus to keep it fully submerged). Lower the heat to medium and allow to gently boil and simmer. Cook for approximately 45 minutes to 1 hour.
While cooking, prepare an ice bath large enough to submerge the finished octopus. Sinks are a preferable choice.
To test the doneness, take a skewer or toothpick and poke the octopus through the thickest part of a tentacle. If the skewer goes through with very little resistance it is done.
Using tongs, remove the octopus and place it into the ice bath. Allow the octopus to cool completely. Once chilled, remove from ice and drain on a kitchen towel (almost the entire octopus is edible except for the beak, unless you are catching fresh).
To remove the beak; take a paring knife and cut out the center of the octopus, or the central area in between all the tentacles under the head. Discard this piece and section the octopus by each tentacle. Allow to dry in the refrigerator for at least an hour.

Potatoes

Place all the cut potatoes into a pot and cover with cool water and salt. Bring water to a boil and then reduce to a simmer. Test the potatoes doneness with a skewer or toothpick, or you can remove a piece and smash with a fork.
You are looking to achieve al dente or a little bite. *Continues on page 99*

WINE PAIRING MARTIN CODAX, Albarino (Pontevedra Spain). With a medium intensity, vibrant and delicious ripe citrus notes and tangerine, this will pair well with the Octopus. Crisp, elegant and fresh with notes of floral such as; jasmine and orange blossom this wine stands up well to the chorizo.

leonora
BISTRO | WINE | TAPAS BAR

Cornmeal & Buttermilk Fried Chicken with Honey and Lemon

CHICKEN
1 whole chicken, cut into 12 pieces

THE WET BATTER
½ gallon buttermilk
7 egg yolks
4 oz Frank's™ redhot hot sauce
1 Tbsp salt, kosher

THE DRY BATTER
2 oz paprika
2 oz coriander, ground
1 oz garlic powder
2 oz onion powder
1 oz oregano, dried
3 oz salt, kosher, to taste
1 tsp cumin, ground
1 oz black pepper, ground
1 lb flour
1 lb cornmeal, finely ground

GARNISH
local honey
lemon zest
hot sauce, your favorite

Chicken
Ask your butcher to cut the chicken into 12 pieces.
If you are brave, break the chicken into 2 wings, 2 drumettes, 2 legs (drums), 2 thighs and 2 breasts (cut the breasts in half for a total of 4 breast pieces)
Place all pieces on towel-lined sheet tray, skin side up, and allow to air dry overnight in refrigerator. You can skip this step if rushed, but we highly recommend that you do not, as it will make the skin less soggy once battered and fried.

Wet Batter
Whisk together the buttermilk, egg yolks, Frank's® Redhot® hot sauce, and kosher salt. Reserve chilled.

Dry Batter
Keep the mix separated to avoid contaminating complete mixture so you can reserve excess for next batch.
Mix in a bowl the paprika, ground coriander, garlic powder, onion powder, dried oregano, kosher salt (to taste), ground cumin, and ground black pepper. Whisk until combined.
In a larger bowl filled with the measured flour and cornmeal, add the spices while whisking to combine. Set aside for next steps.
Note: It is recommended that the dry batter is tasted from tip of finger to determine whether more salt is required. Salt added after chicken is fried won't be enough to compensate.

Dredging Station
Preheat oil to 325 degrees (alternately follow frying stage below). Place the chicken pieces in a large bowl and add dry mix 1 cup at a time. Mix with hands until all pieces are lightly coated (only use as much dry mix to lightly coat). Remember to avoid contaminating – to reserve excess for next batch.
Using 2 separate containers, add dry mix to 1 dish and wet batter to the other dish. Use a sheet tray as the last dish to catch the dredged pieces of chicken. Place mixes in order of dredge (coatings).
Lightly coat chicken pieces – wet batter – dry *Continues on page 99*

WINE PAIRING Lucien Albrecht, Pinot Noir, Cremant d'Alsace (Alsace, France). Crisp and high acidity cuts the richness of the chicken's dark meat and its crunchy crust.
This particular region has been back and forth between French and German rule for centuries. These days there is a cute mix of both cultures. This wine has bright red fruits, a nice tang and life on the palate. Sparkling wine and Fried Chicken are always a solid pairing.

leonora
BISTRO | WINE | TAPAS BAR

The Sebastian Strawberry Snowball

MERINGUE SHELL
10 oz egg white
10 oz sugar
10 oz powdered sugar
1 medium size hemisphere silicon baking mold

VANILLA WHIP
1 qt whipping cream, cold
1 vanilla bean, scraped
1 cup sugar

RASPBERRY DUST
1 lb raspberries, dehydrated or freeze-dried

MICROWAVE CAKE
4 Tbsp flour
½ tsp baking powder
3 Tbsp sugar
½ Tbsp butter, softened
4 Tbsp milk
½ tsp vanilla extract
Pinch of salt

SORBET
4 cups strawberry puree
12 oz sugar
1½ cups half and half

Garnish
Strawberries, quartered
raspberry powder
powdered sugar

Meringue Shell
Whip the whites until foamy, add a third of the sugar and continue whipping until forming soft peaks. Slowly add the remaining sugar while whipping and continue to whip until stiff peaks form. Fold in powdered sugar by hand.
Spray the molds lightly with non-stick spray. Use a spoon and fill the molds with meringue. Spoon out the excess to form a shell shape (thinner for shorter cook time).
Bake at lowest temp your oven will go (ideally 170 degrees fahrenheit) for 1- 2 hours or until dry and crisp. Allow to cool completely before using.

Vanilla Whip
Whisk whipping cream, vanilla bean and sugar in mixer until peaks form. Reserve in fridge until needed.

Raspberry Dust
Finely blend dehydrated raspberries in a coffee grinder or blender. You can crush the raspberries with your fingers. You can always purchase freeze-dried raspberries.

Microwave Cake
In a small bowl, mix together the flour, baking powder, sugar, softened butter, milk and vanilla extract and a pinch of salt. Pour mixture into a 16 ounce, greased ceramic microwave safe mug. Microwave on high for 90 seconds.
Chill and gently break with fingers into 2 inch rough pieces.

Sorbet
Gently melt the sugar. Combine strawberry puree and 'half and half' to melted sugar, then spin in ice cream machine (alternately buy a nice sorbet from the market).

Assembly
Spoon a small amount of vanilla whip onto your dessert plate. Place one half shell open side up on top of the vanilla whip. Make one scoop of sorbet and place inside of open shell. *Continues on page 99*

WINE PAIRING CHÂTEAU MINUTY, "M", *Cinsault, Grenaché, Syrah (Côtes de Provence, France): For a strawberry meringue dessert why not pair with a delicious rosé. This light and bright style of Provencal rosé with flavors on the palate of orange peel and red currant this wine will be a fresh ending to your meal.*

leonora
BISTRO | WINE | TAPAS BAR

Crispy Octopus with Fingerling Potatoes and Chorizo

Crispy Octopus with Fingerling Potatoes and Chorizo, con't from page 96
The potatoes should not fall apart easily.
Remove from water and allow to chill on a sheet tray completely in the refrigerator.

Procedure
In a sauce pan, add minced garlic, olive oil, paprika and chorizo. Gently cook on low heat until the oil has turned red from the chorizo and paprika and garlic looks soft (cook low, there should be no color change on the garlic). Remove from heat, add the lemon juice and half of the parsley. (If oil is too hot, the lemon juice will react with the hot oil. So once again, cook just to warm the ingredients not to sauté. The olive oil is the main liquid component of the sauce and a little goes a long way.)
Toss the chilled potatoes in a little salt and a little oil and reheat as desired (roast in 350 oven for 20 minutes recommended).
Season octopus with salt and grill (or sear with oil in pan) until crispy (can also be flash fried individually with potatoes for 4 minutes).

Assembly
Place the warm potatoes on a platter followed by the octopus tentacles. Drizzle large spoonfuls of the warm chorizo sauce on top of everything.
Garnish with the rest of the parsley and lemon wedges. (warm baguette is recommended for sopping).

E Cornmeal & Buttermilk Fried Chicken with Honey and Lemon

Fried Chicken, con't from page 97 batter (Reserve some dry mix, as mix tends to clump and you may want to start with fresh.
Reserve pieces together by similar parts of chicken. Begin dredging (dredge by similar parts so that is easier to separate for frying stage.) Reserve on sheet tray for frying stage.

Frying Stage
If using tabletop fryer, fry large pieces first as they will take the longest. Do not over crowd the fryer as the chicken will steam and not crisp properly.
If table top fryer is not available, you can shallow fry slowly (325 degrees) in a cast iron pan. Please note that a regular sauté pan is not recommended as it doesn't maintain constant required temperature for frying.
Fry chicken by similar parts (i.e. legs with legs, breasts with breasts, wings with wings), holding each piece at a time to gently swim in oil for 2 seconds so it doesn't stick to the basket. Gently drop each piece into the oil to avoid hot oil splashing back.
Fry until each piece floats to the surface and is golden brown (25-35+minutes for the thickest pieces).

Assembly
Serve chicken with a drizzle of local honey and Lemon Zest and your favorite hot sauce.

Frying Cheat Code
Fry until golden brown, remove from oil and finish cooking in 350 degrees oven.
Place all partial fried pieces together on a sheet tray and bake until internal temp reaches a minimum of 165 degrees fahrenheit. Don't rush and you will get much better results.

The Sebastian Strawberry Snowball

Strawberry Snowball, con't from page 98 Add a second shell, closing off and covering the sorbet. Using a small spoon spread more whipped cream around the entire shell closing off any gaps.
Add 3 or 4 pieces of cake around the snowball.
Add quartered strawberries on top and around the plate.
Sprinkle with raspberry powder and powdered sugar.

LUDWIG'S AT THE SONNENALP

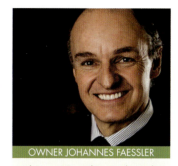

OWNER JOHANNES FAESSLER

Since its Vail opening in 1979, the Sonnenalp has received many accolades and recognition for its achievements from publications including Travel & Leisure and Condé Nast Traveler. The Sonnenalp Hotel in Vail is a member of the prestigious Leading Hotels of the World collection. The Sonnenalp brand has two properties, one in Ofterschwang, Germany and the second in Vail, Colorado. When the Sonnenalp first opened in Germany 100 years ago, Vail wasn't even on the map. The Faesslers envisioned bringing their legacy of European hospitality and superior guest service to the United States and in the 1960's, the burgeoning village at the base of Vail became the ideal location, a renowned, destination intertwined in the fabric of an iconic community. Even though the two hotels are a world apart, they share a welcoming spirit cultivated by a history of family ownership and management that makes staying at the Sonnenalp an unforgettable resort experience.

Ludwig's Breakfast finds its origin in the Sonnenalp Hotel's long tradition as a ski lodge and the understanding that no meal is more important before heading out for a day on the slopes. The Sonnenalp combines the European Breakfast tradition of breads, cold cuts, cheeses, home baked pastries, fruit and Muesli with the wonderful dishes typically found in Colorado like eggs, bacon, pancakes, waffles (along with a few healthy items!) and so much more.

Ludwig's Breakfast is served in a way where everyone gets to choose their favorites, and where guests can determine their own pace from being in a hurry to get to the slopes to getting the day started nice and slow.

Visit Ludwig's Breakfast for the distinguishing year-round terrace (glass covered and heated during winter) and enjoy this truly unique and wonderful creek-side setting in the middle of Vail Village.

Johannes Faessler graduated from the University of Denver in 1984. He is the owner of the Sonnenalp Hotel in Vail, Colorado. Johannes is the fourth generation in his family to manage the Sonnenalp and prides himself on continuing in his parents, grandparents and great grandparents' footsteps as he continuously transforms the Vail Valley hotel. Along with his wife, Rosana, and their children, the family has set and maintained the highest standards of hospitality and service.

LUDWIG'S
Bavarian Eggs Benedict

POACHED EGGS
1 tsp table salt, to taste
2 Tbsp white vinegar
4 large eggs, each cracked into a small handled cup
ground black pepper

ADDITIONAL
German rye bread or heavy dark bread
black forest ham
fresh dill for garnish

HOLLANDAISE SAUCE
12 Tbsp unsalted butter, softened
6 large egg yolks
½ cup boiling water
2 tsp lemon juice
⅛ tsp cayenne pepper
1 tsp tomato past
salt

Poached eggs
Fill an 8 to 10 inch nonstick skillet nearly to the rim with water. Add 1 teaspoon salt and the vinegar, and bring mixture to boil over high heat.

Lower the lips of each cup into water. Tip eggs into boiling water, cover, and remove from heat. Poach until yolks are medium-firm, exactly 4 minutes. For firmer yolks (or for extra large or jumbo eggs), poach 4½ minutes; for looser yolks (or for medium eggs), poach 3 minutes.

With slotted spoon, carefully lift and drain each egg over skillet. Season to taste with salt and pepper and serve immediately.

Hollandaise Sauce
In large heat-resistant bowl, whisk the butter and egg yolks together then set over medium saucepan with ½ inch of barely simmering water (don't let bowl touch water) until mixture is smooth and homogeneous.

Slowly add ½ cup boiling water and cook, whisking constantly, until thickened and sauce registers 160 degrees on instant-read thermometer (7 to 10 minutes). Remove from heat, stir in lemon juice, tomato paste and cayenne pepper. Season with salt to taste.

German Rye Toast and Black Forest Ham
Toast German Rye bread (a heavy dark bread substitute will do) to liking. Sauté Black Forest ham (2 minutes per side over a medium high heat).

Assembly
Assemble for presentation, starting with the toast as your base, then the cooked ham, poached egg at the center of each slice of toast. Then ladle over the top of the eggs a generous portion of hollandaise.

Garnish
Garnish with fresh dill.

COCTAIL PAIRING *STRAWBERRY COCKTAIL. Muddled Strawberries, 1.5 Gin, .25 Honey, .25 Lemon Juice, .25 Demerara (Simple Syrup), topped with Champagne). Brunch food needs brunch cocktails. A perfect pairing to add some extra flavor: Botanicals from the Gin, acid from the Lemon, sweetness from the honey, and fruit from the strawberries. The Champagne to help balance the Cayenne flavoring quite nicely.*

Sonnenalp Ham & Cheese Quiche

QUICHE FILLING
1½ cup, chopped deli ham
½ cup, shredded cheddar
½ cup, shredded Monterey Jack
2 green onions, thinly sliced
¾ cup heavy cream

6 large eggs
½ tsp Kosher salt
¼ tsp freshly ground black pepper

PIE CRUST
3 cups pastry flour
1 tsp salt

½ cup shortening
½ cup cold butter
½ cup ice cold water
1 Tbsp white vinegar

Preheat oven to 375 degrees.

Quiche Filling
Mix together the chopped ham, shredded cheddar, Monterey Jack and sliced green onions.
In a large bowl, whisk together the heavy cream, eggs, salt, and pepper.

Pie Crust
Sift the flour and salt into a large bowl. Cut in the shortening and the butter until the mixture resembles coarse crumbs.
Mix the water and vinegar together in a cup. Add this liquid mixture to the crumbs. Mix together just until the dough is combined and handles well.
Sprinkle flour on the counter before rolling out the dough. Split the dough into two chunks.
Roll out one piece on a floured surface. Roll the dough about ½ an inch larger than your pie pan.
Press dough into a 9" pie plate and crimp edges. Line crust with parchment paper and fill with dried beans or pie weights. Bake until lightly golden and set, about 15 minutes. Remove pie weights and bake 5 minutes more until bottom crust is golden. Let cool slightly.

Assembly
Scatter ham, cheddar, Monterey Jack, and green onions in bottom of the golden pie crust. Pour egg mixture over the ham and cheese filling in pie crust.
Bake until just set in the center, about 40 minutes.
Let cool 15 minutes before slicing.

COCKTAIL PAIRING GRAPEFRUIT BELLINI *Grapefruit juice, a popular juice to have for breakfast and brunch. Instead of a Peach Bellini, we chose the Grapefruit version to pair with the quiche and will add a nice citrus quality to your meal. The ham, and the cheese are rich components of the dish and the acid from the fresh Grapefruit purée will cut through those flavors well.*

PIE WEIGHTS *hold down the dough. This helps in preventing airpockets as well as hold the shape against the pie plate.*

Ludwig's Waffles

WAFFLE
1⅓ cups flour
4 tsp baking powder
½ tsp salt
2 Tbsp sugar
2 eggs, separated
½ cup butter, melted
1¾ cups milk

TOPPINGS
maple syrup, small pitcher
1 cup strawberries, sliced
1 cup raspberries, sliced
1 cup powder sugar
4 Tbsp butter

Waffle
In a large mixing bowl, whisk together the flour, baking powder, salt and sugar.

In a small mixing bowl, separate the eggs. Add only the yolks to the dry ingredient mixture, leaving the whites in the small bowl.

Beat the egg whites until moderately stiff; set aside.

Add milk and melted butter to dry ingredients and egg yolk mixture, and blend well.

Fold stiff egg whites into mixture.

Ladle mixture into hot waffle iron and bake.

Assembly
Serve immediately.

Top with a pat of butter and berries or favorite fruit topping. Sprinkle with powdered sugar. And the final step is your favorite maple syrup drizzled on top.

Bon Appetit!

WINE PAIRING VEUVE CLIQUOT, Reims, (Champagne, France) NV: Champagne and Waffles go together like Tostitos and Salsa. This pairing is for someone who wants to feel as if they are kings and queens eating a waffle at brunch. Veuve is a perfect pairing because of the brioche (toast) flavors that pair well with the waffle. The Raspberry and strawberry toppings will help accentuate the flavors of this Champagne quite nicely.

LUDWIG'S
Sonnenalp Chocolate Croissants

CROISSANT DOUGH
- ¼ cup (4 Tbsp) unsalted butter, softened to room temperature
- 4 cups all-purpose flour, plus more for rolling/shaping
- ¼ cup granulated sugar
- 2 tsp salt
- 1 Tbsp active dry or instant yeast
- 1½ cups cold whole milk
- 1 4-ounce bar semi-sweet or bittersweet chocolate, coarsely chopped
- confectioners' sugar for dusting (optional)

BUTTER LAYER
- 1½ cups (3 sticks) unsalted butter, softened to room temperature
- 2 Tbsp all-purpose flour

EGG WASH
- 1 large egg
- 2 Tbsp whole milk

Croissant Dough
In a mixer with a dough hook, add butter, flour, sugar, salt, and yeast and on low-medium speed gently combine for 1 minute. Keep mixing and slowly adding all the milk. Increase speed to medium-high and beat for 5 full minutes. (If you don't have a mixer, knead by hand for 5 minutes). The dough should be soft and pull away from the sides of the bowl. The dough is ready when it bounces back after poking the surface with your finger.

Remove the dough from the bowl with floured hands and work it into a ball. Place the dough on a lightly floured silicone baking mat, parchment paper, or baking sheet.

Gently flatten the dough and cover with plastic wrap or aluminum foil. Refrigerate for 30 minutes.

Shape the Dough
Remove the dough from the refrigerator, transfer it to a lightly floured surface. Flatten with your hands and rolling pin, working the edges into a 14 × 10-inch rectangle. Place the dough rectangle back onto the baking sheet. Cover with and place back into the refrigerator for 4 hours, overnight or up to 24 hours.

Butter Layer
Prepare the butter layer 35 minutes prior to laminating the dough to allow time to chill.

In a large bowl, beat the butter and flour together using a mixer with a paddle or whisk attachment until smooth. Transfer the mixture to a silicone baking mat, or parchment paper.

Using a small spatula, spread the butter mixture into a 7 × 10-inch rectangle. Transfer the mat or paper with the butter layer onto a baking sheet. Refrigerate for 30 minutes or until the butter is firm, but still pliable. If too firm, laminating the butter layer within the dough in the next step will be difficult.

Laminate the Dough
Remove the dough and butter layer from the refrigerator. Place the dough on a lightly floured counter; flatten again to a 14 × 10-inch rectangle, if needed. Center the *Continues on page 110*

DRINK PAIRING ESPRESSO AU CHOCOLAT *An Espresso with a bit of Chocolate added into it is an incredible idea to pair with this dish. Any restaurant HAS to have chocolate sauce. Make sure to dip the Croissant into the Espresso (or coffee) for an extra delicious experience.*

TIPS *Croissants taste best the same day they're baked. Cover any leftover croissants and store at room temperature for a few days or in the refrigerator for up to one week. You can also freeze for up to 3 months.*

Ⓐ Sonnenalp Chocolate Croissants

Chocolate Croissants from page 109 butter layer on the dough and fold each end of the dough over the butter. If the butter wasn't an exact 7 × 10-inch rectangle, use a pizza cutter or sharp knife to even out the edges. Seal the dough edges over the butter layer with your fingers.

Roll the butter/dough layers into a 10 × 20-inch rectangle. Fold lengthwise into thirds as if you were folding a letter. Place the folded dough on the baking sheet, cover. Refrigerate for 30 minutes.

Remove the dough from the refrigerator, place the short end facing you, and repeat the steps of rolling dough into a 10 x 20-inch rectangle two more times, placing into the refrigerator to cool between turn. After the third turn, refrigerate for 4 hours or overnight.

Shape the Croissants

Remove the chilled dough from the refrigerator. On a lightly floured surface, roll the dough into an 8 × 20 inch rectangle. The dough will be firm and want to be oval shaped. Work the dough with your hands and rolling pin until you have the correct size rectangle. Using a pizza cutter or sharp knife, slice the dough in half vertically. Each skinny rectangle will be 4 inches wide. Then cut 3 even slices horizontally, yielding 8 – 4 × 5-inch rectangles. Cut each rectangle in half lengthwise so you have 16 – 2 × 5-inch rectangles.

Working with one rectangle at a time, use your fingers or a rolling pin to stretch dough to about 8 inches long. Do this gently as you do not want to flatten the layers. Place a few small pieces of chocolate in a single layer at one end and tightly roll the dough up around the chocolate.

Repeat with the remaining dough, placing the shaped croissants, end seam down, on 2 lined baking sheets, 8 per sheet. Loosely cover and allow to rest at room temperature for 30 minutes, then place in the refrigerator to rest for 1 hour or up to 3 hours.

Assembly

Preheat oven to 400 degrees. Whisk the egg and milk together for the egg wash. Remove the croissants from the refrigerator. Immediately brush each lightly with egg wash and place into the oven. Bake until golden brown, about 20 minutes, rotating pans halfway through baking. If croissants start darkening too quickly, reduce the oven to 375 degrees.

Remove the croissants from the oven. Place on a wire rack to cool slightly before serving. Dust with confectioners' sugar before serving.

Sonnenalp Acai Bowl with Homemade Granola

ACAI PURÉE
1 cup of apple juice
1 large banana, sliced
1½ cups frozen berries
½ cup vanilla Greek yogurt
1 Tbsp honey
1 frozen packet of acai berry puree (¾ cup), broken into pieces

GARNISH TOPPINGS
assorted toppings such as sliced almonds, berries, shredded coconut, Sonnenalp homemade granola, chia seeds, sliced banana, mint sprigs, etc.

SONNENALP HOMEMADE GRANOLA
1½ cups sunflower seeds
1¼ cups pumpkin seeds
1½ cups pecans
5¼ cups oats
¼ cup black sesame seeds
1¼ cups honey
2 cups maple syrup
¾ cup coconut oil
1 Tbsp vanilla paste
1 tsp ground cinnamon
½ cup coconut flakes

Pre-heat oven to 285 degrees.

Acai Berry Purée
Place the apple juice, banana, frozen berries, yogurt, honey and acai puree in the blender.
Blend until thoroughly combined and smooth.

Sonnenalp Homemade Granola
In a large mixing bowl, combine the Sunflower Seeds, Pumpkin seeds, pecans, oats, black sesame seeds, honey, maple Syrup, coconut oil, vanilla paste, ground cinnamon and coconut flakes.
Mix ingredients together and spread out on large baking sheet and bake for 25 minutes at 285 degrees.

Assembly
Pour the smoothie into 2 deep bowls.
Arrange the desired toppings over your smoothie bowls and serve.

WINE PAIRING Mimosa. While some people may think that this is an easy pairing I find that a Mimosa is just what the bartender ordered. Considering you are trying to be a bit healthier with your breakfast choices you might want to be a little "naughty" and enjoy some delicious sparkling wine and some OJ.

ACAI BERRY Known to be a rich antioxidant which is deep purple in color and comes from the acai palm tree, native to Central and South America.

MIRABELLE

BC

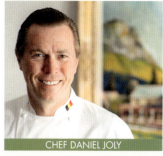

CHEF DANIEL JOLY

We welcome you to 119 years of history, our historic landmark and our proud family-owned restaurant.
Mirabelle at Beaver Creek is the original homestead in Beaver Creek. The west wing of the restaurant and the barn to the east were built in 1898. In 1981, the rear portion of the building, including the kitchen, was added. 1982 marked the opening of both the Beaver Creek Ski Resort and Mirabelle.

My wife Nathalie and I arrived in 1991 as general manager and executive chef, respectively. We converted the top level of the farmhouse into a bedroom and raised our family in this very building.

Cuisine, Wine List and Awards…
Our wine list offers over 350 selections from all over the world with an emphasis on French and California wine. Prices for a full bottle of wine range from thirty seven to four thousand five hundred dollars. Peter Casey, our wine director, has curated our list since we arrived at Mirabelle in 1991.
Our many awards and accolades have come from DIRONA, MOBILE, AAA, Wine Spectator, Travel and Leisure, and James Beard. Those and others are displayed downstairs in the restaurant.

Although our origins are from the past, our focus is on innovation and the future. In the last few years, 2017-2019, we've added the back patio alongside the stream. In addition, we have remodeled the bar and lounge area to make it more cozy, put on a new roof, repainted the inside and out, added new carpet for the whole restaurant and built a greenhouse behind the kitchen. Currently, summer of 2019, we are re-tiling the entire kitchen and wait station. All the while, we are trying to stay true to our historical heritage. Mirabelle has its own parking lot and is accessible thru the Dial-a-Ride service in Beaver Creek.

Born in Brussels, Chef Daniel Joly studied at Brussels Culinary School. In 1988, he was awarded "The Best Young Chef" in Belgium. After working at 3-star Michelin restaurant Comme Chez Soi, Chef Daniel and his wife, Nathalie, moved to Folly Beach, South Carolina where he was chef at Restaurant Million in Charleston, SC.

In 1991, Mirabelle was run by chef Daniel and Nathalie and in 1999 they purchased Mirabelle. In 2016, after 17 years of trying, they purchased the land surrounding the restaurant. "I feel fortunate to have found Mirabelle as it has been a great stage for me to express myself professionally. With the help of my staff and my family we continue to have fun working toward our original goal of a owning a great restaurant in amazing Colorado!"

Seared Jumbo Scallop Colorado Summer Corn Alysa Purée with Prosciutto Dust

SCALLOPS
12 large diver sea scallops

CORN PURÉE
6 Colorado fresh corn
4 large onion
1½ tsp of pepper flakes (spice)
12 large diver sea scallop
½ cup of butter, unsalted

GARNISH
baby micro green
1 russet potato
deep fry oil
sea salt, to taste
4 slices of prosciutto ham de Parma

Corn Purée
Clean the corn and remove the leave and all corn hair with the help of a clean, dry towel. Using a sharp knife, remove the corn kernel from the cob, reserving all corn in a large bowl.

Using a large sauté pan, add unsalted butter, enough to sauté the onion. Let the onions cook until translucent. Add the corn, pepper flakes and a pinch of sea salt to taste.
Simmer for 15 minutes on low heat. Stir the corn mixture with a wooden spatula to insure it's evenly cooked.
When cooked, use a blender or food processor to puree the mixture, add salt and pepper to taste and continue to blend for few more minutes to get a smooth puree. Be careful the corn mixture will still be hot, so open the lid carefully to slowly release the steam. Add a spoonful of unsalted butter to the puree. Set mixture aside while you cook the scallops.

Scallops
In a heated pan, to sear the scallops, about 1-3 minutes on each side or until cooked through.

Potato Garnish
I like to garnish this dish with our fun crispy potato ball.
To create this, we use a turn slicer, also known as a spiral slicer or spiralizer, to create long strings of potato.
Using a small basket, stainless steel tea infuser, fill it with the potato strings and dip fry them at 375 degrees for about 4 minutes or until golden brown.
Open and remove the potato ball from the infuser.

Prosciutto Ham de Parma Garnish
I use a slice of Parma ham and set in a silpat and dry it in the oven at 120 degrees for about an 1 hour to get crispy Parma ham chips. Break the crispy chips into small pieces. Add that salty and crunchy element to the dish. Finish with micro greens.

WINE PAIRING LUMINUS, Chardonnay, (Napa Valley, California) 2015. A lighter Chardonnay with a vibrant brightness about it. Aromas of oak, and silky smooth richness added to the mid-palate with hints of lemon zest and orange peel to hold up against the "flavor blast" of this dish.

SILPATS are non-stick baking sheets. They are a blend of food-safe silicone and a fiberglass mesh which creates a versatile non-stick surface. They are reusable and work at a very wide temperature range.

Ravioli with Carrot Honey Lavender, Confit of Duck, Colorado Goat Cheese Cream and Brussels Sprout Leave Salad

CARROT MUSSELINE
4 big carrots
3½ oz unsalted butter
4 yellow onions, clean and sliced
2 sprigs of fresh lavender
   (lavender bag if fresh is not available)
2 Tbsp honey
salt and ground pepper, to taste
cumin, to taste

PASTA DOUGH
4 cups of organic all purpose flour
¼ cup duck fat, melted
⅔ cup of water
1 tsp salt

DUCK CONFIT
4 duck legs
1 cup sea salt
1 cup sugar
½ cup, fresh thyme
1 qt duck fat

COLORADO GOAT CHEESE CREAM
¼ cup goat cheese
¾ cup heavy cream
salt and pepper, to taste

BRUSSELS SPROUT
3 cups of Brussels sprout leaves
2 Tbsp duck fat

Carrot Mousseline
In a quart pan, boil water with a pinch of salt. Create a sachet with the lavender and cook to add the lavender flavor to the water. Remove the sachet, add the carrots and onions. Cook until tender. Strain, add 2 tablespoons of honey, then pass through a ricer or puree in a blender. Add unsalted butter, salt, pepper and cumin to taste. Set aside to cool then fill into a pastry bag.

Pasta Dough
In a small Kitchen Aid or mixer, combine the flour, ¼ cup of melted duck fat, ⅔ cup of water, and 1 tsp salt. Mix until you have a nice and smooth dough. Do not over mix. Wrap in plastic film and set in the cooler

Duck Confit
Preheat oven to 225 degrees.
In a bowl mix the sugar, sea salt and thyme. Pour the mixture on top of the duck legs. Keep mixture for 6 hours to soak the flavor. Then rinse under cold water and dry with paper towel. Melt the duck fat in a medium heat. Lay the duck legs in a baking dish with high sides. Pour the melted duck fat over the duck legs and cook for 4 hours at 225 degrees until soft and tender. It is important not to over- heat *Continues on page 124*

WINE PAIRING KAMEN, *Cabernet Sauvignon, Moon Mountain District, (Sonoma, California) 2014. I absolutely love a phenomenal duck dish. My first pick is to pair this dish with a 1986 Ducru Beaucaillou (a marvelous Chateau, and vintage from Bordeaux). When that isn't available a delicious California Cabernet is the next best thing. I first learned about Kamen a few years ago and I find their silky smooth Cabernet absolutely stunning. The flavor blast of raspberry, licorice, chocolate, and forest floor are the next best thing to a 33 year old Bordeaux.*

Organic Free-Range Chicken Breast (sous vide) in Olive Oil, with Apple Gratin Potatoes

CHICKEN BREAST
6 chicken breasts, 6-7 oz each
2 cups extra virgin olive oil
½ garlic clove, cleaned and chopped
1¾ Tbsp sea salt
1 Tbsp coarse black pepper
1 cup of fresh rosemary
1 cup of fresh thyme

APPLE GRATIN POTATOES
4 large Yukon gold potato pellet, sliced thinly
1 lb of unsalted butter, melted
4 golden apples, peeled, sliced thinly
grated nutmeg
salt and pepper to taste
thyme flower
clarified butter

CRANBERRY COMPOTE (Garnish)
½ lb fresh cranberries
1 Tbsp grated orange zest
1 tsp grated lemon zest
¼ cup fresh orange juice
3 Tbsp fresh lemon juice
½ cup granulated sugar
1 tsp pure vanilla extract
2 cups water
3 Tbsp cornstarch

THYME INFUSE OLIVE OIL
1 qt olive oil
1 lb of thyme flower

BEURRE NOISETTE
butter

BELGIAN WAFFLE (alternate side)
2¼ cup of Yukon potato puree
1 oz thyme infused virgin olive oil
⅓ cup all-purpose flour
1½ tsp sea salt
¾ tsp ground pepper
⅓ tsp ground nutmeg

GARNISH
cranberry compote
baby micro greens

Chicken Breast
In a large bowl, mix the chicken breasts, garlic, sea salt, coarse black pepper, fresh rosemary, fresh thyme and olive oil.
Using plastic sous vide bags, vacuum seal the breast with the olive oil and herbs blend; do not vacuum set your vacuum at level 6 so as not to over-do the vacuum pressure. Give the chicken breast room to infuse some of the good flavor from the olive oil and fresh herbs. *"I love olive oil, and chicken is a big part of my childhood and gives me that magical feeling."*

In a water circulator (sous vide), set at 145 degrees, poach your chicken in the bag for 90 minutes. The *sous vide process with chicken adds flavor and tenderness to the meat*
When your chicken is fully cooked, set the bag in ice cold water to stop the cooking process and chill the meat.

Apple Gratin Potatoes (Belgian waffle for alternate side dish).
Thinly slice the potatoes and apples. Then, in a flat pan, alternate the potato and apple to create layers.   *Continues on page 123*

WINE PAIRING VAN DUZER *Pinot Noir, (Willamette Valley, Oregon) 2015 A producer on the verge of having a sub appellation named after it would be the perfect choice to pair with this chicken dish. The Van Duzer corridor, a prominent part of the Oregon Wine Trail is legendary with its western wind that flows through the gap and into the Willamette Valley. The wild strawberry and herbal notes that go-along with this wine are absolutely amazing with this chicken dish. There is also a lengthy finish to make sure you still get a bit of flavor for the entire meal through the Gratin Potatoes.*

Colorado Peach Cream Cheese Cake

COLORADO PEACH CREAM CHEESE
3 large ripe Palisade Colorado peaches
¾ cups Philadelphia cream cheese
1 cup heavy cream, cold
1½ Tbsp powdered sugar
2⅓ oz granulated sugar
4 pc gelatin sheet
1 egg yolk

MERINGUE
1 cup egg whites
2 cups sugar

CARAMEL
1 cup brown sugar

MACADAMIA NUT POWDER
½ cup macadamia nut
2¾ Tbsp mountain honey
¾ Tbsp of brown sugar

GARNISH
1 sprig of mint (garnish)

Colorado Peach Cream Cheese (gluten free and delicious)
Warm the cream cheese in a bain-marie (double boiler). Pre-soak the gelatin sheet (pre-soaking the gelatin helps prevent a lumpy mixture). Mix the gelatin in with the cream cheese until it dissolves evenly. Add the granulated sugar and mix all together. Using a Kitchen Aid, add the egg yolks to the mixture and whip to aerate and create a mousse.
In separate bowl, whip the cold heavy cream with the powdered sugar until light and firm then add to the cream cheese. In a form mold, add slices of peach first and the cream mixture on top. Refrigerate for 2 hours before use.

Caramel
In a sauce pan, on medium heat, add a thin layer of the brown sugar and heat. As the sugar begins to melt you can add a bit more, gently mixing the new sugar into the melted sugar (do not stir to vigorously). This process happens fast to keep an eye on the pan. You don't want to burn the sugar and have to start over.

Macadamia Nut Powder
Use a mixer or blender to blend the brown sugar, macadamia nuts and honey to create a honey nut dust. Dry it using the silpat until ready to use.

Meringue
In a blender, whip 1 cup of egg whites and 2 cups of sugar until firm.
Using a baking sheet and a silpat, with a spatula, lay the meringue about ¼ inch thick. Let the meringue dry in the oven at 120 degrees.
Dry for 2 hours until dry and break in large pieces.

Assembly
Spread the caramel across your dessert plates. Dust the caramel with the macadamia nut powder. Finish with a piece of Colorado peach cream cheese cake.
Garnish the top with a dry piece of meringue and fresh mint.

WINE PAIRING CHATEAU LIONS DE SUDUIRAUT, Sauternes, (Bordeaux, France) 2012. This sweet wine producer of Bordeaux makes a delicious and delectable dessert wine pairing exponentially well with any and all desserts, cheesecake being one of the best. The honeysuckle, and apricot flavors of the wine are a perfect to give it a hint of acid when adding the richness of the cheesecake.

COLORADO PEACH CREAM CHEESE: Let me tell you about the summer in Beaver creek. We can write a book and probably have a lot to say. One real sign of summer in Colorado is the Palisade peach from the valley. And they are just perfect! …so let's give them homage here.

Mirabelle
At Beaver Creek

Mirabelle Cookie Assortment

CANNELES BORDELAIS (about 20 pieces)
1 vanilla bean
2 cups of whole milk
1¾ oz unsalted butter
2 whole eggs
2 egg yolks
1 cup of sugar
1½ Tbsp of good rum
¾ cup all-purpose flour, sifted

FINANCIER
2 cups powdered sugar
1¾ cups almond flour
1¾ cups all-purpose flour
1½ tsp baking powder
9 egg whites
1½ cups unsalted butter noisette

ROCHER COCO
½ cup whole milk
1¼ cups sugar
2¾ cups coconut shaving
2 ⅓ Tbsp flour
4 whole eggs

HAZELNUT COOKIE
1 cup unsalted butter
¾ cup sugar
1½ Tbsp vanilla paste
1¾ cups all-purpose flour
1 cup quality hazelnut powder (flour)

MACAROON
2 cups almond powder
1¾ cups powder sugar
7 egg whites
1 cup sugar

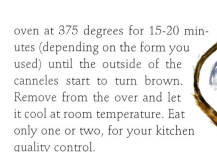

Preheat oven to 375 degrees.

Canneles Bordelais
Best to prepare the cookie batter a day before you bake them to amplify flavor and final results.
Split the vanilla bean in half lengthwise.
In an inox casserole, boil the milk with the split vanilla bean, let it infuse for 1 hour and set aside.
In a separate pan, melt the unsalted butter. Remember not to over-melt the butter.
In a large bowl, whisk the whole eggs and yolks. Add the sugar, melted butter, sifted flour and rum. Whisk evenly.
Add the milk-infused vanilla bean (strain before using). Let the liquid cool down.
Using flexi or form pan or mold for the Canneles, cook in warm oven at 375 degrees for 15-20 minutes (depending on the form you used) until the outside of the canneles start to turn brown. Remove from the over and let it cool at room temperature. Eat only one or two, for your kitchen quality control.

Financier
In a mixer, whisk the egg whites until light and aerated. Add almond flour, all purpose flour, powdered sugar and baking soda. Lastly, add the melted butter.
Let rest in the cooler for 1 hour and bake at 375 degrees for 15 minutes until golden in color.

Continues on page 124

DRINK PAIRING MONTENEGRO Amaro (on the rocks, with an orange twist, (Italian Liqueur). If you can get a bottle of Montenegro, or any Amaro for that matter, I would highly recommend it as a pairing. While it may not be wine it will certainly be the right ending after a wonderful meal experience. Amaro, which is an Italian liqueur is perfect for an after dinner digestif. The roots and herbs that are fermented and put together for this drink are a perfect "stomach settler", and with the ice and orange twist really bring out amazing qualities.

Mirabelle
At Beaver Creek

🅔 Organic Free-Range Chicken Breast (sous vide) in Olive Oil

Organic free-range chicken and Belfian Waffle, con't from page 120

Season with salt, pepper, nutmeg, and thyme flower.
Pour clarified butter to cover your gratin, place in the oven and cook for 45 minute at 350 degrees.

Clarified Butter
Melt the butter in a 1 quart pan over low heat. Do not stir until melted and butter is separated into solids and fats.
Remove from the heat and let stand for 5 minutes.
Skim off the foam then slowly pour off clear yellow liquid leaving the milk solids in the pan. Store the clear yellow liquid in the refrigerator.

Beurre Noisette
In a sauté pan melt butter whisking gently as it melts, monitor to prevent burning. The butter will start to foam then begin browning. Once it starts to brown, remove from heat to cool down to stop any further cooking and burning. Use it immediately or refrigerate for use later, but only gently reheat.

Cranberry Compote
Combine in a medium-size nonreactive saucepan, over medium-high heat, the cranberries, orange and lemon zest, orange and lemon juices, sugar, vanilla, and 1½ cups of the water. Bring to a boil and cook for 8 minutes.
Dissolve the cornstarch in the remaining ½ cup of water and add to the pan. Reduce the heat to medium, then stir constantly until the mixture thickens, about 2 minutes.
Remove from the heat and cool completely.

Thyme Infuse Olive Oil
Combine the olive oil and thyme at least day prior to use. Let infuse for a day at room temperature and strain using a strainer.

Belgium Waffle (but not the one you think!)
Can not be a Belgian if we don't have a waffle…. as much as Belgian people eat sweet waffle in the street and fair at anytime of the day, we play with the waffle recipe to create a salty and mostly potato based waffle to compliment our chicken dish or beef tenderloin. Also best paired with any red meat or fish. Use chopped fresh herbs to compliment and add freshness to the dish.
This is a great alternate side dish for any entrée. Try it with Mirabelle's scallop dish as well.
In a mixing bowl, combine the all purpose flour, sea salt, ground pepper, and ground nutmeg.
Peel the potato then cook and strain trough a ricer to finely puree the potato.
Combine the potato and dry ingredient and mix well.

Belgium Waffle
Using a waffle iron on medium heat, cook the waffles until golden brown.

Assembly
When you are ready, warm the chicken breast with beurre noisette in a pan cook till golden brown. Using a plate, set the warm apple and potato gratin and add the chicken and garnish with cranberry compote and baby micro green. Belgian Waffle can be substituted in as a side dish for this dish.

Serves 6-8.

Mirabelle
At Beaver Creek

ⓢ Ravioli with Carrot Honey Lavender, Confit of Duck, Colorado Goat Cheese (cont'd)

Raviolo with Carrot Honey Lavender, con't from page 119

the fat while cooking the duck legs, slow medium heat is best. Strain the fat from the duck confit, and using your hand, pull the meat off the bone and take the skin off. Only keep the meat (you can keep the fat and re-use for another duck confit process later). Make sure you strain it well and keep in a container with a lid for future use.

Ravioli
Using a pasta machine, thinly slice the pasta to level 8-9 with a 2 inch metal circle.
With a pastry bag, place a bit of the carrot mousseline on top of one pasta circle. Use a pastry or clean paint brush and, with water, apply to the edge of the pasta dough circle. Use another pasta circle for the top and seal the edges of the pasta to make a complete ravioli. Reserve until ready to cook.

In a large pot with boiling water add a pinch of salt. Boil the ravioli for 4 minutes until the pasta is cooked. Set on a plate with butter.

Colorado Goat Cheese Cream
In a Vitamix or blender, blend the goat cheese and cream. Season with salt and pepper.

Brussels Sprout with Duck Confit
Using a large sauté pan with little duck fat, sauté the Brussels sprout leaves and the pulled duck confit.

Assembly
On a plate, set goat cheese cream; add the warm duck, Brussels sprout leaves, salad and carrot mousseline ravioli.

Mirabelle Cookie Assortment (cont'd)

Mirabelle Cookie Assortment con't from page 122

Rocher coco
In a large bowl, mix the coconut, flour, sugar and whole eggs, and gradually add the warm milk. Mix all together and with your hand, make a ball about half inch diameter. Set on a silpat in a tray, cook at 375 degrees in the oven for 5 minutes until golden in color.

Hazelnut cookie
Using a Kitchen Aid mixer, mix butter, sugar, vanilla and hazelnut together. Gradually add the flour until incorporated. Place the mixture on a pan and place in the refrigerator to keep cool. Once cooled and firm, use a small, round cookie cutter to cut the cookie dough in circles. Place on a pan with parchment paper and bake for 4-6 minutes at 375 degrees.

Macaroon
Whip white eggs with sugar until stiff, add the almond powder and sugar. Mix gently until incorporated. Using a spatula, set the mixture in pastry bag. In a baking sheet with a parchment paper, create a 1 inch diameter macaroon. Let it dry and rest for 15 minutes. Bake at 400 degrees for 6 minutes. Remove from the oven and let it cool so that they can be separated nicely. Macaroon can be put together with jam or pastry cream. Also, you can add colors to your macaroon. You can add essence of lemon or pistachio. The sky's the limit …

SPLENDIDO AT THE CHATEAU

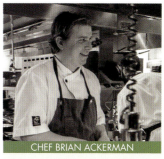

CHEF BRIAN ACKERMAN

The remarkable location and timeless elegance of Splendido has made it one of Colorado's most elevated dining destinations for decades. The restaurant was opened at the Chateau Beaver Creek in the early 1990's and most recently reimagined in 2016 by Executive Chef Owner, Brian Ackerman. The restaurant was updated that year to delight guests with its inviting mountain chic atmosphere.

Year after year, Ackerman and his team continue to offer impeccable service and a dynamic wine list that all tastefully align with an innovative and seasonally inspired menu of contemporary American cuisine.

The drive up to Splendido always feels a bit like an introduction to an idyllic fairy tale. Pull through a stone archway to arrive at the door and be immediately welcomed by gracious hosts and the grand foyer of the Chateau. From the start of every Splendido evening until the sweet finale, the talent, passion and hospitality of this establishment are what make truly delicious memories.
So many of Splendido's best offerings never go out of style. You can always enjoy a perfect dish of Dover Sole and never be disappointed, or sit in awe while your fork cuts with barely an ounce of pressure into a beautiful cut of Foie Gras.

Adjacent to the dining room, the charming piano bar and lounge area pairs perfectly with a lighter bite of oysters and a martini or a succulent burger with a glass of Bordeaux.
As with the creation of all great art, it's a constant flow of inspiration and innovation that feeds the artists. Every night while the Splendido pianist is serenading a dining room full of guests, Ackerman leads his team in a production drawn from classic and contemporary, the old and the new.

Chef Brian has been with Splendido for over a decade, working as a sous chef and then as chef-de-cuisine. He purchased the restaurant in the spring of 2016, and as executive chef he is committed to carrying on the restaurant's pronounced legacy within the Colorado culinary scene. Brian focuses on the highest quality ingredients, with creative yet streamlined preparations so food is always presented in pure and delicious renditions.

Starting his studies in restaurant management at the University of Missouri, Brian completed his training at the Culinary Institute of America in Hyde Park, New York. Following graduation, he worked under notable chefs, including Ken Oringer (of Toro and Uni acclaim). After moving to the Vail Valley, he helped chef Kelly Liken open her namesake restaurant in Vail Village.

Elk Carpaccio

ELK CARPACCIO
8 oz elk tenderloin
2 Tbsp pine nuts
2 oz smoked Pecorino
¼ cup Arugula
1 Tbsp vegetable oil
olive oil, to taste
Maldon salt*
applewood smoke chips

BLACK GARLIC AIOLI
10 black garlic cloves
1 egg yolk
1 Tbsp Dijon mustard
1 Tbsp lemon juice
1 Tbsp sherry vinegar
2 cups vegetable oil
kosher salt, to taste
black pepper, to taste

PICKLED CHANTERELLES
3 cups white wine vinegar
1 cup water
¼ cup sugar
⅛ cup salt
2 Tbsp mustard seed
1 Tbsp black peppercorn
3 bay leaf
1 sprig thyme
1 sprig sage
1 sprig dill
2½ lbs chanterelle buttons, quartered

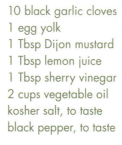

Elk Carpaccio
Trim fat and silver skin from elk tenderloin. In a cast iron pan lightly sear the elk, caramelizing each side in vegetable oil. Let rest for 10 minutes.
Cold smoke the elk tenderloin with applewood for one hour. Wrap elk in plastic wrap and freeze for one hour.
Remove from the freezer then slice the elk very thin and place flat on plate. A slicer is recommended.

Black Garlic Aioli
Combine and blend black garlic cloves, egg yolk, Dijon mustard, lemon juice and sherry vinegar in food processor until smooth – about 90 seconds. Scrape down sides.
Slowly add the vegetable oil to emulsify. Season with salt and pepper. Adjust consistency by adding cold water as needed.

Pickled Chanterelles
Combine the white wine vinegar, water, sugar, salt, mustard seed, black peppercorn, bay leaf, thyme, sage, and dill and bring to a boil. Place chanterelles in a stainless steel bowl and pour in hot pickling liquid. Allow the Chanterelles to marinate for at least 1 hour at room temperature. Note: Chanterelles have a 6 week refrigerated shelf life.

Assembly
Place elk on a plate and drizzle with olive oil.
Toast pine nuts and scatter evenly.
Shave smoked pecorino with peeler and scatter with baby arugula. Sprinkle Maldon salt.
Slice and place pickled chanterelles.
Finish with dollops of black garlic aioli.

WINE PAIRING ADELSHIEM Pinot Noir, (Willamette Valley, Oregon) 2017. With the cooler climate in Oregon most of their Pinot Noirs have a lighter body than their California counter-parts. This wine has a delicious flavor of ripe red berries, some slight tannin, but a wonderful fruit flavor profile throughout the entire glass. A staple on many wine lists throughout the country and a perfect pairing for this dish.

*__MALDON SALT__ is an English sea-salt from Maldon, England. The salt flakes are thin, uneven, and crunchy and provide a more clean, and pure salt taste. Better as a table finishing salt used sparingly rather than in cooking.

Porcini Soup

PORCINI SOUP
¼ lb Butter
1 onion, chopped
1 leek, white part only, chopped
1 celery stalk, chopped
½ bulb garlic, cut in half

1 lb fresh Porcini mushrooms, cleaned & chopped fine
1 gallon chicken stock
¼ gallon cream
cayenne pepper, a pinch
kosher salt and black pepper, to taste

SACHET
cheesecloth
1 Tbsp whole black peppercorns
5 sprigs fresh thyme
handful of parsley stems
2 bay leaves.

In a stock pot, sweat the onion, leek, celery, and garlic in the butter over medium heat without coloring.
Add the chopped porcini mushrooms and continue to cook for about 15 minutes, stirring often.
Add the chicken stock and sachet to the stock pot, bring to a simmer and cook for about 30 minutes.
Remove the sachet, purée the soup in a blender in batches, then strain through a fine chinois, returning the soup to a clean stock pot.
Add the cream and bring back to a simmer.
Season the soup with salt, black pepper and a pinch of cayenne.
Strain the soup again through the fine chinois.
Taste & serve.

Sachet
Place the fresh thyme sprigs, parsley stems, bay leaves and whole black peppercorns in the center of a square of cheesecloth. Gather up the corners of the cheesecloth and tie off in a bundle leaving long leftover string on both ends to tie to the handler of the pot for easy extraction when done. Make sure to cut any really long ends after tying to pot to avoid a fire hazard.

Serves 6

WINE PAIRING PASCAL JOLIVET Sancerre (Loire Valley, France) 2017. This producer, which hails from the Loire Valley of France, makes spectacular Sancerre (this is actually 100% Sauvignon Blanc, but named after the sub-region the wine is made is called Sancerre). With the higher acid and the vibrant flavors of pineapple, mango, and guava, this wine will help bring some brightness to this dish. The amount of cream and butter makes this dish quite rich. The freshness of this wine will help balance out the Porcini soup nicely.

Colorado Rack of Lamb

COLORADO RACK OF LAMB
(3) 8 bone Racks of Colorado Lamb, French cut*

POMEGRANATE MARINADE
1 qt pomegranate juice
¾ cup olive oil
2 lemon, juice and zest
5 shallots, chopped

12 garlic cloves, chopped
2 Tbsp rosemary, chopped
1 Tbsp thyme, chopped
1 Tbsp black peppercorns, crushed

Prepare this dish a day in advance to give lamb 24 hours to marinate.

Pomegranate Marinade
Combine the pomegranate juice, olive oil, lemon juice and zest, chopped shallots, garlic, rosemary, thyme, and crushed black peppercorns in large container.

Place racks of lamb in marinade for 24 hours.
Remove and place on sheet tray.

French Chops
Score the lamb chops across all the rib bones on each side where the meat thins out to create a clean cut and to expose the rib bones leaving the bulk of the meat on the bone. Do this on both sides cutting the meat between the ribs as you go so you can peel off the meat from the ribs.

Lamb Preparation
Once French cut* lamb chops have marinated over night, wrap the bone ends in foil. Season with salt and pepper.
Roast in a wood oven, high temperature oven or grill until caramelized.

Turn heat down to 350 degrees and roast to desired temperature (approximately 15 minutes for medium-rare to medium).
Rest for at least 20 minutes.
Slice & serve.

Serves 6

WINE PAIRING CHATEAU BEAUCASTEL, *Chateauneuf du Pape (Rhone Valley, France) 2005. Chateauneuf du Pape tend to be a bit harsh when they are younger. These wines are meant to age for quite sometime. Once aged they have an amazing palate of dark rich fruits with a hint of savory notes. Enjoy the aromas of blackberry jam, liquorice, and an array of spice notes.*

***FRENCH CUT LAMB CHOPS** Bones that have the meat cut away from the ends of the ribs so the end part of the bone is fully exposed for a more elegant look to your meal.. You can usually find lamb racks already french cut in the market or your local butcher can prepare the lamb rack this way for you.*

Splendido
AT THE CHATEAU

Alaskan King Crab Fettuccine

ALASKAN KING CRAB
1 lb Alaskan King Crab, cooked, deshelled
1 tsp chives, chopped
fresh cracked black peppercorn, to taste

PRESERVED MEYER LEMON
1 star anise
1 cardamom pod
¼ tsp black peppercorns
¼ tsp fennel seeds
¼ tsp coriander seeds
¼ tsp cumin seeds
4 Meyer lemon*, washed & dried
½ cup kosher salt
⅛ cup sugar
1 pinch red pepper flakes
fresh lemon juice
1 qt Mason jar

FETTUCCINE
5 egg yolks
1 whole egg
1¼ cups all purpose flour
1 pinch salt

BEURRE BLANC
1 cup white wine
¼ cup shallots, brunoise
½ cup Champagne vinegar
1 tsp peppercorn
2 sprigs thyme
2 sprigs parsley
1 bay leaf
1 lb cold unsalted butter, diced
salt & white pepper, to taste
fresh lemon Juice, to taste

Preserved Meyer Lemon
Create a dry spice mixture by combining, star anise, cardamom pod, black peppercorns, fennel seeds, coriander seeds and cumin seeds and toast in skillet. Add the salt, sugar & a pinch of red pepper flakes into the spice mixture.
Score each Meyer lemon* ¾ each direction then place the first lemon in mason jar and sprinkle with the dry spice mixture. Repeat layering lemons and mixture while pressing lemons down. Add lemon juice if space allows.
Apply a lid and store in refrigerator for up to 3 days prior to use. They will have a 6-month shelf life.

Fettuccine Pasta
Combine egg yolks, whole eggs, flour and salt in a bowl, food processor or a standard mixer. Work the ingredients together until they are integrated, and the dough holds together.
Turn the dough out onto a clean work surface and knead until it is smooth and no longer sticky, 10 to 15 minutes. If the dough is sticky, add a little more flour. If you use a mixer, switch to the dough hook attachment and knead the dough until it is smooth, about 7 minutes, again adding flour if necessary.
Wrap the dough in plastic wrap and set aside at room temperature for at least 40 minutes or refrigerate it overnight.
Allow the dough to come to room temperature *Continues on page 135*

WINE PAIRING ETUDE, Carneros (Sonoma County, California) 2017. Etude makes a particularly delicious California Chardonnay with a bright and citrusy flavor profile. Everyone automatically assumes that all California Chardonnays are buttery and oaky, however, there are some great producers that go against the grain.

*MEYER LEMONS will be sweeter then your everyday lemon. They are smaller, rounder and smoother, with a thinner skin and deeper yellow to orange color. The key note here is that for cooking, Meyer lemons are less tangy as regular lemons which gives you a much sweeter taste. The scent of the rind is more complex scent than regular lemons — more like an herb or a spice.

Lemon, Fennel, Olive Oil

LEMON CUSTARD
⅓ cup lemon purée
¾ cup sugar
2 egg yolks
2 egg whites
⅙ cup custard powder
½ cup butter

LEMON SORBET
¾ cup lemon puree
1½ cups water
¾ cup sugar
½ tsp Trimoline*
½ tsp stabilizer
¼ cup glucose powder

FENNEL GRANITA
½ cup white fennel, chopped
⅛ cup green fennel, chopped
4¼ Tbsp water
4¼ Tbsp sugar syrup
2 tsp lemon juice or puree

FENNEL CRISP
¼ cup sugar
1¾ Tbsp glucose
1 tsp butter
4 Tbsp almond meal
1 tsp fennel powder

FENNEL CRUMBLE
3 Tbsp butter
2 Tbsp sugar
2 Tbsp brown sugar
¼ cup almond meal
½ tsp salt
½ tsp fennel powder

OLIVE OIL GEL
3 Tbsp sugar
4 tsp water
½ tsp glucose
¼ tsp gelatin
1⅓ Tbsp olive oil

Lemon Custard
In a food processor, blitz lemon purée, sugar, egg yolks, egg whites and custard powder together, then strain it through a chinois.
Cook in bain marie, or double boiler, until 185 degrees fahrenheit. Let cool for a bit and incorporate room temperature butter. Mix well. Store in piping bag in refrigerator.

Lemon Sorbet
Heat water with trimoline* in sauce pan then add the sugar, stabilizer and glucose powder.
Allow to boil, then pour over lemon purée in mixing bowl. Strain mixture through a chinois. Rest overnight in covered container. Churn the next day.

Fennel Granita
Combine the white fennel, green fennel, water, sugar syrup, and lemon juice or purée in a food processor and blitz thoroughly. Strain through chinois.
Freeze the mixture overnight, then grate with a fork the next day. Store in freezer.

Continues on page 135

WINE PAIRING VILLA RUSSIZ, Pinot Grigio (Collio, Italy) 2017. "Collio" in Italian means "hillside", which is exactly where this vineyard is located. The vineyard sits on slope with large amount of sun which gives the wine that hint of guava, passionfruit, and mango. The cool air that comes from the lake at night also gives it a bright acidity to pair well with the fennel.

TRIMOLINE Also known as invert syrup is a viscous liquid. Compared to sucrose, this sugar is sweeter and its products (glucose and fructose) tend to retain moisture and are less prone to crystallization. Most of the sugar in honey is also inverted sugar.

Crab Fettuccini (cont'd)

Crab Fettuccini; con't from page 133 before you roll it out. Roll and cut the dough into the desired shape and cook in boiling salted water until it is just tender.

Beurre Blanc
Reduce the white wine with the shallots, champagne vinegar, peppercorn, thyme, parsley, and bay leaf in a non-reactive pan. Over medium heat, slowly whisk in the cold butter, one tablespoon at a time, allowing the butter to emulsify and become warm before adding more. Continue until all the butter has been added and the sauce is very warm. Do not allow sauce to boil or cool as it will break.

Season with salt, pepper and lemon juice, then strain. Keep in a warm place.

Assembly
Rinse preserved lemons & discard insides.
Chop zest very fine, then in a stainless-steel pot over low heat combine the lemon zest with ¼ cup of beurre blanc.
Add Alaskan king crab and pasta to the pot and toss.
Add additional beurre blanc as desired.
Sprinkle with chives and black pepper.

Serves 6

Lemon, Fennel, Olive Oil (cont'd)

Lemon, Fennel, Olive Oil; con't from page 134

Fennel Crisp
Boil sugar, glucose and butter until golden color. Add almond meal and fennel powder and mix well.
As it cools, roll out finely between parchment paper, then, once set, break with a rolling pin.
With a food processor, blitz into powder, then sift finely onto parchment paper.
Cook at 320 degrees for a few minutes until caramel color.
Let cool, then break into small pieces.

Fennel Crumble
Cut butter into small cubes and mix with sugar, brown sugar, almond meal, salt and fennel powder until butter is incorporated. Flatten mixture out onto cookie sheet and cook at 350 degrees, checking every few minutes until golden color.
When done chop into crumbles

Olive Oil Gel
Start by tempering the gelatin. To prevent clumpy gelatin soak it in a small amount of cold water or another cool liquid. Once hydrated the gelatin will dissolve easily ready to use.
Boil sugar, water and glucose. Add tempered gelatin to warm mixture and put into a food processor.
Incorporate olive oil very gently, like making mayonnaise.
Store in piping bag.

Assembly
Start layering with 3 tablespoons of lemon custard in a bowl.
Cover with 2 tablespoons of fennel crumble.
Next add 1 tablespoon of fennel crisp.
Then add 1 tablespoon swirl of olive oil gel.
Cover with 3 tablespoons of fennel granita.
Finish with 1 scoop of lemon sorbet.

Serves 6.

SWISS CHALET

EXECUTIVE CHEF ALEJANDRO ROJAS

The Swiss Chalet Restaurant first opened its doors in 1986 as part of the opening of the Swiss Hotel, one of three hotels owned and operated by the Sonnenalp family in Vail that year.

As part of the overall Swiss theme, the restaurant was built with authentic Swiss-Alpine design in mind. The Swiss Chalet was created in a way to transport guests to Europe. Everything inside the restaurant was carefully curated and considered, including all furniture, decorations (many Swiss cowbells), china, and even the uniforms worn by the restaurant waitstaff.

Swiss-born Peter Boden, a long-time Vail resident, joined the Sonnenalp as Swiss Chalet Chef de Cuisine and helped create a truly authentic menu made up of dishes typical for the Alpine Region in Switzerland, which our current chef, Alejandro Rojas, continues in the tradition. These dishes included a variety of fondue and raclette items – items that still make up the foundation of the Swiss Chalet's menu. The restaurant was an immediate success and continued operations in the Swiss Hotel location until 2004 when the hotel was demolished.

The Swiss Chalet Restaurant then moved a block west into a new, bigger location specially designed for this unique restaurant as part of the Sonnenalp Hotel where it can be found today. These design elements included adding a patio and special ventilation for all that raclette and cheese!

The focus on authentic alpine cuisine prepared to the original Swiss recipes, made with the correct ingredients, remains the main focus of the Swiss Chalet. In order to retain this focus, all the restaurant's cheese is imported for freshness and authenticity. This is incredibly important as the Swiss Chalet uses roughly 1,600 pounds of cheese in one month!

The Swiss Chalet not only offers an authentic alpine experience, but gives families and friends alike a chance to bond in the cozy comfortable space. Families and diners of all ages continue to make this now over 30-year tradition a 'must do' during their Vail vacation.

Chef Alejandro graduated from the Culinary Program at The Art Institute of Houston and has over 20 years of hospitality experience including owning his own restaurant, Wok Playa, in Mexico, serving Southeast Asian food with a Latin twist.

Alejandro has served as Executive Chef at the Rosewood Hotel and Resort in Mayakoba, alongside top chefs – Massimo Bottura, Daniel Boulud and Enrique Olvera. He worked under Hugo Ortega, to open Hugo's Restaurant, and under chef Tim Keating at the Four Seasons, Quattro Restaurant, both in Houston. In 2010, Alejandro served as the Executive Chef at the Mandarin Oriental Riviera Maya under chef Ignacio Granda. In the early 2000's, studying the cuisine of the Yucatan Peninsula, Alejandro opened the restaurant at the SLH Hotel Esencia, and was invited to cook at the James Beard House in New York.

Käse Fondue

SLURRY
½ oz corn starch
½ oz Kirsch

KÄSE FONDUE
1¼ cup dry white wine
2 cloves garlic, minced
10 oz Appenzeller Cheese, grated
10 oz Vacherin Cheese, grated
½ oz Kirsch
small pinch nutmeg
salt & pepper to taste

CONDIMENTS
1-2 baguettes
broccoli
cornichons
apples
favorite fruits or vegetables

Käse Fondue
Start with your slurry mixture. Mix corn starch and Kirsch to equal parts and set aside.
In the fondue pot, heat the white wine and garlic over medium heat. Slowly add the cheeses and the Kirsch. Increase the heat to melt the cheese while constantly stirring ingredients into a smooth mass.

Finally, slowly add the slurry, nutmeg, salt and pepper until you have stabilized the cheese fondue to the perfect consistency.

Set the fondue pot on a fondue pot burner so it stays hot throughout your dinner.

Fondue Condiments
Cut baguette into cubes.
Additional vegetables as, broccoli, cornichons etc. as well as any fruits, apples that you might enjoy with your fondue.

WINE PAIRING *JEAN-RENE GERMANIER Fendant Vétroz (Valais, Switzerland) 2017. The staple entrée at the Swiss Chalet deserves the wine best paired with it, a Swiss Fendant. This fresh white wine compliments many cheeses and goes especially well with Fondue. Alternately, we recommend a crisp, dry Riesling from Germany as great wine pairing.*

SWISS CHALET
Züricher Geschnetzeltes

VEAL
1¼ lb veal top round
½ Tbsp white flour
2 Tbsp sunflower oil
salt and pepper to taste

SAUCE
2 Tbsp butter
¼ onion, finely chopped
2 cups sliced mushrooms
½ cup dry, white wine
¾ cup demi-glace
½ cup heavy cream
½ Tbsp chopped parsley
salt and pepper to taste

Veal
Cut veal into thin slices.
Prepare a plate with flour and dust the veal with flour.
Heat sunflower oil in a pan.
Add veal and quickly fry until browned on both sides. Remove the veal from the pan onto a plate, season with salt and pepper and set aside.

In the same pan you used to fry the veal, add butter and finely chopped onions and cook for 2 minutes.
Add the sliced mushrooms to the onion mixture and cook until mushrooms are soft.

Sauce
Pour in the white wine to deglaze the bottom of the pan and reduce until half of the wine remains.
Stir in the demi-glace.
Add the whipped heavy cream and cook until you have a creamy consistency.
Add the veal to the sauce and heat, but do not let boil.
Add salt and pepper to taste and top with chopped parsley.

Assembly
Serve with Potato Rösti or Spaetzle. See following pages for Swiss Chalet Rösti or Spaetzle side dish recipes.

Serves 4 people.

WINE PAIRING FERRARI-CARANO Tré Terre Chardonnay (Russian River, California) 2016. For this dish, I enjoy a Chardonnay with some weight but as an alternative, another interesting pairing would be a Rhone-blend such as Michel Chapoutier "Petite Ruche" Red, Crozes-Hermitage, France 2014.

Potato Rösti

POTATO RÖSTI
1 lb Yukon Gold potatoes, peeled
1 tsp cornstarch
salt and white pepper to taste
2-3 Tbsp clarified butter

Potato Rösti
Grate the peeled potatoes coarsely.
Mix potatoes with cornstarch and season with salt and white pepper.
Divide grated potatoes into 2 equal portions.
Heat up a large cast iron skillet or non-stick pan over medium heat and melt 1 tablespoon of clarified butter.
Add one portion of potatoes to pan and flatten to shape into a compact cake.
Cook the rösti for 5-6 minutes on both sides, or until golden brown on both sides and tender in the inside.
Add more butter as necessary.
Repeat the process with the second portion of potatoes.
Optional: Brush with melted butter.

Serves 4 people.

WINE PAIRING *Domäne Wachau Gruner Veltliner Terrassen Federspiel (Wachau, Austria) 2017. As a blank canvas to work with, traditionally this would pair well with the Gruner Veltliner but in a different direction. The Potato Rosti would also go great with a cool-climate Pinot Noir. My choice for a Pinot Noir would be Lingua Franca Estate Pinot Noir Eola-Amity Hills, Oregon 2016.*

RÖSTI OR RÖÖSCHTI *A Swiss dish consisting of potatoes, similar to a fritter. Originally a breakfast dish, from the canton of Bern, this is a favorite served throughout Switzerland and around the world.*

SWISS CHALET
Käsespätzle

SPAETZLE
1 cup all-purpose flour
3 eggs
1½ Tbsp milk
1½ Tbsp water
1 tsp salt
pinch nutmeg
1½ Tbsp butter

CRISPY ONIONS
½ yellow onion, sliced into very thin rings
1 Tbsp cornstarch
salt, to taste
vegetable oil for frying

CHEESE SAUCE
1 Tbsp butter
½ yellow onion, diced
½ cup of heavy cream
1 cup Gruyère, grated
½ cup Vacherin cheese, grated
½ cup Appenzeller cheese, grated
salt and pepper to taste
2 tsp chopped parsley

Spaetzle
Sift the flour into a large bowl. Mix the eggs, milk, water, salt, and nutmeg into the sifted flour.
Beat the batter until bubbles begin to form on the surface of the batter.
To cook the spaetzle, bring water to a boil in a large pot and add a little bit of salt.
Press the batter through a spaetzle maker into the boiling water a few tablespoons at a time. You can also use a large hole grater or colander as an alternative.
Cook until spaetzle rises to the surface and is tender.
Drain and toss with butter.

Crispy Onions
Toss sliced onions in cornstarch and salt.
Heat a few tablespoons of vegetable oil in a pan, enough oil to be able to fry the onions.
Deep fry the onions until golden brown. Set on paper towels to drain excess oil.

Cheese Sauce
On medium heat, add butter and sauté the diced onions in a pan.
Add spaetzle and heavy cream and bring to a boil.
Add cheeses and stir until cheese is melted.
Season with salt and pepper.
Top with chopped parsley and crispy onions.

Serves 4 people.

WINE PAIRING DR. LOOSEN, RIESLING (MOSEL, GERMANY) 2016. *A crisp Riesling from either the Reingau or Mosel.*

Apfelstrudel (Apple Strudel)

PASTRY DOUGH
3 oz strudel dough
1-2 tsp flour

STRUDEL FILLING
1 Tbsp butter, melted
2 Tbsp breadcrumbs
1 lb of apples, peeled and cored
3 Tbsp sugar
1½ Tbsp hazelnuts, ground
1 Tbsp of raisins
½ tsp cinnamon

ASSEMBLY
2 Tbsp lemon juice
1 Tbsp butter, melted

VANILLA SAUCE
½ cup milk
½ cup heavy cream
2 egg yolks
3½ Tbsp sugar
½ vanilla bean

GARNISH
1 Tbsp butter, melted
1 tsp powdered sugar

Preheat the oven to 460 degrees.

Strudel Filling
Mix the breadcrumbs with 1 tablespoon of butter and toast in oven for a few minutes until golden. Set aside.
Cut peeled and cored apples into thin slices. Mix with one tablespoon of lemon juice. Set aside.
Mix sugar, hazelnuts, raisins, cinnamon, and remaining lemon juice and set aside.

Pastry Dough
Sprinkle flour onto a pastry cloth. Roll out strudel dough until paper thin to about 8" x 26", being careful not to rip the dough.

Assembly
Cover two-thirds of the dough with the toasted breadcrumbs, sliced apples, and sugar mixture. Brush the last third of the dough with melted butter.
Begin to roll the strudel with the help of the pastry cloth, rolling from the side with toppings to the buttered side.
Line a baking sheet with parchment paper and place the strudel on the sheet, seam side down.
Brush strudel with butter and bake for 15 minutes until golden.

Vanilla Sauce
Heat milk, heavy cream, and vanilla in a saucepan over medium heat and bring to a boil. Remove from heat.
In a separate bowl, whisk the egg yolks and sugar together.
Add the milk mixture into egg yolk mixture and whisk to combine. Return mixture back to the saucepan and heat over low-medium heat, whisking until the mixture is at 180 degrees and thick enough to cover the back of a spoon.
Pour the sauce through a fine-mesh strainer.
Serve warm over Apple Strudel.

Garnish
After cooking, brush again with melted butter, sprinkle with powdered sugar and cut into slices. Serve with warm vanilla sauce.

Serves 4 people.

WINE PAIRING KRACHER Scheurebe Trockenbeerenauslese (Burgenland, Austria) 2010. Feel free to pair this traditional apple pastry with a dessert wine, try a Sauternes or Tokaji, but I prefer this dish with the KRACHER Scheurebe Trockenbeerenauslese.

TERRA BISTRO

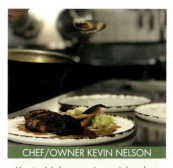

CHEF/OWNER KEVIN NELSON

For dining in Vail, Terra Bistro has been an essential experience since its opening day in 1991. Right out of the gate Terra Bistro made a splash with adventurous cuisine, mountain-casual décor, and true hospitality. With a long-standing dedication to organic ingredients and environmental stewardship, Terra Bistro set the trend before the organic farm to table movement became a standard for quality cuisine. Meanwhile, decades of accolades have piled up from Zagat, DiRoNa, Wine Spectator, James Beard, TripAdvisor, Opentable, the Vail Daily, the Denver Post, the New York Times, and more. Terra Bistro consistently holds a place as a top recommendation among Vail's dining scene and remains a local's hot-spot to this day. Ever changing seasonal menus have produced many signature favorites such as Coriander Spiced Tuna with Tamari Vinaigrette, Luxardo-Adobo Glazed Pork Chops, and Brick Chicken with French Onion Confit. Add to that, an extensive award-winning wine list and playful craft cocktails such as the "Kombucharita", "Peachy Keen", and "Words Cannot Espresso", and you'll see why Terra Bistro can not be missed.

Find Terra Bistro inside of the Vail Mountain Lodge located at the east end of Vail Village, just steps away from Gore Creek and the Vail Village parking structure. We're sure to be a highlight of your visit to Vail.

Kevin Nelson, a Long Island transplant, was hired on at Terra Bistro in 1993 as a Chef's Apprentice and took over as Executive Chef and General Manager in 1999. Under Chef Nelson, Terra Bistro quickly secured its place among a short list of must-do dining spots in Vail Village. In 2006, Chef Nelson became Terra Bistro's managing partner. Along the way, Terra Bistro became known for Chef Nelson's innovative flavor combinations and his lighter approach to quality cuisine. When building his seasonal menus, Chef Nelson aims to connect with his guests through a playful approach to familiar yet decidedly unconventional concepts.

Baked Ricotta with Tomato Jam, Fennel Sausage, and Garlic Toast

RICOTTA CHEESE
16 oz heavy cream
1 gallon whole milk
3 oz white vinegar
2 Tbsp salt
2 Tbsp sugar

TOMATO JAM
1½ lb vine ripe tomatoes; cored, roughly chopped
1½ lbs cherry tomatoes, quartered
2 cups white sugar
2 oz lemon juice
1 Tbsp ginger, peeled, grated on a box grate
2 tsp crushed red pepper flakes
1 tsp salt
½ tsp cinnamon
¼ tsp ground cumin

FENNEL SAUSAGE
5 lbs ground pork (coarsely ground)
½ cup whole fennel seed
½ cup ground fennel seed
¼ cup paprika
¼ cup garlic powder
4 oranges, zested
4 Tbsp salt
4 Tbsp sugar
4 Tbsp ground black pepper
1 cup ice cold water

GARLIC TOAST
1 baguette, sliced ¼" thick on a bias
8 oz butter, softened
1 tsp garlic powder
2 Tbsp garlic, minced
2 Tbsp parsley, chopped
½ tsp fresh oregano, chopped
¼ tsp crushed red pepper flakes
¼ cup grated Parmesan

Garnish
crushed pepper flakes

Ricotta Cheese

Place milk, cream, sugar, and salt in a pot and bring to a boil. Be careful as to not allow the mixture to boil over. As soon as the mixture comes to a boil, add vinegar and simmer for another one to two minutes. Place cheesecloth in a colander and place the colander in a bowl with enough space between the bowl and the colander to collect liquid (this is the whey). Carefully ladle out cheese curds into colander lined with the cheesecloth. Allow cheese curds to drain and cool in the refrigerator for at least two hours.

After at least two hours, place only the curds in a food processor and puree until smooth. While pureeing, add whey (the liquid that has collected in the bowl beneath the colander), if necessary, to achieve desired consistency. The final product should be smooth and slightly looser than cream cheese. Makes 2 quarts of ricotta.

Tomato Jam

Combine the tomatoes, cherry tomatoes, sugar, lemon juice, ginger, red pepper flakes, salt, cinnamon, and ground cumin in a sauce pot and bring to a boil. Stir the jam frequently to avoid scorching on the bottom of the pot. Reduce to a simmer and cook until mixture thickens (approximately one to one and a half hours), continuing to stir every so often. *Continues on page 157*

WINE PAIRING RUNQUIST '1448' Red Blend (California) 2016. You will want a red wine with weight, spice, and jammy fruit. A zinfandel blend with a little residual sugar will help combat the salty and spicy characters of this dish without overpowering it.

Turmeric and Coconut Cauliflower Soup

TURMERIC CAULIFLOWER SOUP
2 cups white or yellow onion, roughly chopped
¼ cup oil (olive, canola, safflower, or any neutral vegetable oil)
12 cups cauliflower, florets and stems divided
6 cups vegetable stock (or water)
2 Tbsp brown sugar

4 cups coconut milk
⅛ tsp cayenne
½ Tbsp lime juice
1 orange, juiced
1 tsp ground cardamom
1 tsp ground turmeric
1 tsp ground cumin
¼ cup fresh ginger, peeled and minced

GARNISH
shredded dried coconut
toasted pumpkin seeds
chives, thinly sliced

In a large pot or Dutch oven, heat oil over medium to low heat, then add chopped onions. Cook the onions, stirring occasionally, until translucent.

Once the onions are translucent and have softened, add 8 cups of cauliflower and cook until both florets and stems have softened.

Once the cauliflower has softened, add the vegetable stock (or water), brown sugar, coconut milk, cayenne, lime juice, orange juice, cardamom, turmeric, cumin, and ginger to the pot. Bring soup to a boil, lower heat to low, and simmer for approximately 45 minutes.

Add the remaining 4 cups of cauliflower and simmer for an additional 15 minutes. Allow the soup to cool slightly, then using a blender, puree in batches until soup has a very fine and smooth consistency. Strain the soup through a fine sieve, and season to taste with salt.

To Serve
Ladle hot soup into warm bowls and garnish each bowl of soup with shredded coconut, pumpkin seeds, and chives.

Makes 3 quarts of soup.

WINE PAIRING *Chalk Hill Chardonnay (Sonoma, California) 2017*

Seared Scottish Salmon with Green Goddess Hummus and Zhoug

SALMON
4-6 oz Scottish salmon pieces, skin removed
pomegranate seeds, for garnish

GREEN GODDESS HUMMUS
5 cups dried chickpeas (soaked overnight)
1 tsp baking soda
6½ cups water
10½ oz tahini paste
6 Tbsp lemon juice
4 garlic cloves, crushed
2 oz olive oil
2 cups parsley leaves; loosely packed, rough chopped
½ cup tarragon; loosely packed, rough chopped
¼ cup chives, rough chopped
¼ cup green onions, rough chopped
6½ Tbsp ice cold water
1½ tsp salt

ZHOUG
1½ bunches cilantro; leaves and stems
1 cup carrot tops, large stems removed
½ cup parsley, large stems removed
8 jalapenos; remove seeds, rough chopped
½ tsp crushed red pepper flakes (to taste)
⅛ tsp ground cardamom
½ tsp coriander seeds
½ tsp cumin seeds
1 Tbsp pumpkin seeds
4 garlic cloves, roughly chopped
1 tsp salt
½ tsp ground black pepper
4 oz olive oil
1 Tbsp lemon juice

VEGETABLES
brocolini or asparagus

GARNISH
pomegranate seeds
lemon oil

Green Goddess Hummus

Wash 5 cups of chickpeas. In 1½ gallons of water, soak the dried chickpeas over night. The beans will quadruple in size. Blend tahini (be sure to stir the paste before measuring) and lemon juice in a blender until combined. Add garlic, olive oil, herbs, and onions and blend until vivid green paste forms. Be careful not to heat the mixture too much in the blender.
Drain chickpeas from soaking liquid.
Over medium heat, cook the chickpeas and baking soda for 3 minutes, stirring constantly, until outer skins of chickpeas begin to peel away from the bean. Add water to chickpeas and bring to a boil, then reduce to a simmer. Cook chickpeas for 30 to 35 minutes, skimming off all scum as it rises to the surface. The finished cooked beans should be tender but not mushy. Drain chickpeas, place in a food processor, and process until stiff paste forms. Be sure to scrape down the sides of the bowl, as needed.
Once stiff, smooth paste is achieved, add the tahini/herb mixture to chickpeas, along with 1½ teaspoons of salt.
While the food processor is running, slowly drizzle in the ice cold water and continue to mix for five minutes until smooth and creamy.
Transfer the hummus to a bowl, press plastic *Continues on page 157*

WINE PAIRING La val Albarino (Rias Baxias, Spain) 2017. This is a sauvignon blanc wine with tropical flavors, salinity, and medium weight. Ask your local wine shop for a classic Albarino. Most Albarino wines will give the acidity and brightness that this dish needs.

Tres Leches Shortcake with Caramel-Rum Sauce and Sweetened Whipped Cream

TRES LECHES SHORTCAKE
3 cups all-purpose flour
½ tsp baking soda
½ tsp baking powder
½ tsp salt
8 oz butter, room temperature
2⅓ cups white sugar
4 eggs
1 tsp vanilla
8 oz buttermilk

½ can evaporated milk
5 oz whole milk
1 cinnamon stick
1 cloves
½ can sweetened condensed milk
½ tsp vanilla
¼ tsp cinnamon

CARAMEL-RUM SAUCE
1 can sweetened condensed milk
2 oz cream
1 oz dark rum

SWEETENED WHIPPED CREAM
1 pint heavy whipping cream
½ Tbsp vanilla
2 Tbsp powdered sugar

Prep
Preheat oven to 350 degrees and prepare pan by buttering a half sheet tray. Cover the bottom of the tray with a piece of parchment paper and butter the parchment, ensuring the sides of the tray are also buttered.

Batter – Dry Ingredients
In a mixing bowl, combine flour, baking soda, baking powder, and salt and set aside.

Batter – Wet Ingredients
Using a stand up mixer with the paddle attachment, cream butter and sugar at medium speed until light and fluffy. After each stage make sure to scrape down the sides and bottom of the bowl.
Add eggs, one at a time, allowing each egg to be mixed in before adding the next. Mix in the vanilla. Once wet ingredients are blended well, alternate adding between the dry ingredients and buttermilk (start with the dry ingredients, e.g. dry, buttermilk, dry) until mixed well. Do not to over mix.

Tres Leches Shortcake
Pour batter into prepared pan and smooth the top. Place on middle rack and bake 35 to 40 minutes, until center is done and cake begins to pull away from the sides. Allow the cake to cool for 20 minutes then turn onto cooling rack.

Cake Filling
Have two mixing bowls ready for this stage.
In the first mixing bowl, place milk,

Continues on page 158

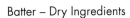

WINE PAIRING Royal Tokaji, 5 Puttonyos (Hungary) 2008. Tokaji is a classic Hungarian dessert wine with caramel undertones and enough sweetness to compliment this dessert without adding acidity

Kombucharita

SPICY JALAPENO TEQUILA
1 bottle silver or blanco tequila
2-3 fresh jalapenos

SPICY SALT RIM
1 Tbsp smoked paprika

1 Tbsp cayenne pepper
1 Tbsp salt
1 Tbsp white pepper
1 Tbsp sugar
fresh lime and dip into salt mixture.

2 oz jalapeno tequila
½ oz orange liqueur (Cointreau)
½ oz fresh lime juice
¼ oz agave syrup
ice
2-3 oz of your favorite kombucha flavor

Spicy Jalapeno Tequila
Make a few slits with a sharp knife in each jalapeno and add them to a glass jar with the tequila. Allow to infuse for at least 24 hours (longer if you prefer a more powerful kick!) and then remove jalapenos.

Spicy Salt Rim
Combine the smoked paprika, cayenne pepper, salt, white pepper, and sugar. Rim your glass using a fresh lime and dip into salt mixture.

Terra Bistro Kombucharita
Combine your homemade jalapeno tequila, orange liqueur (like Cointreau), fresh lime juice and agave syrup in a cocktail shaker; add ice and shake hard until fully combined. Pour into salt rimmed tall glass and top with 2-3 ounces of your preferred flavor of kombucha.

Spicy jalapeno infused tequila gets a healthy kick! Our signature Terra Bistro margarita topped with your favorite flavor of kombucha. Serve tall with a housemade salt rim.

ⓐ Baked Ricotta with Tomato Jam, Fennel Sausage, and Garlic Toast (cont'd)

Baked Ricotta, con't from page 152 Once the jam thickens, remove from heat, place in another container and cool. Makes 1½ quarts of jam.

Fennel Sausage

Combine the ground pork, fennel seed, paprika, garlic powder, orange zest, salt, sugar, black pepper and water in a large mixing bowl and mix well. Cook a little pinch of the sausage to check for seasoning. Season with more salt, if needed. In a hot skillet, sear off half teaspoon sized bits of sausage until cooked through. Remove sausage bits from the pan and cool on a plate or sheet tray lined with paper towels.

Garlic Toast

To make garlic butter, combine butter, garlic powder, garlic, parsley, oregano, crushed red pepper flakes, and Parmesan and mix until well combined. This recipe will make about 1 cup of garlic butter.

While the garlic butter is still soft, spread enough butter to cover the top surface of each slice of baguette. Preheat the oven to 425 degree oven, place pieces of baguette on a baking sheet tray and toast garlic bread for approximately three minutes, or until the edges of the bread start to turn golden.

Assembly

In 425 degree oven, using individual, ovenproof, soufflé baking dishes, place approximately three ounces of ricotta cheese and one ounce of tomato jam in the ovenproof dish and bake for five minutes. Remove from the oven, sprinkle with crushed red pepper flakes, and serve with toasted garlic toast.

ⓔ Seared Scottish Salmon with Green Goddess Hummus and Zhoug (cont'd)

Seated Scottish Salmon, con't from page 154 directly to the surface, and allow to rest for at least 30 minutes.

Zhoug

Wash cilantro, carrot tops, and parsley in cold water and dry thoroughly in salad spinner or rolled up in a kitchen towel. Toast coriander seeds, cumin seeds, and pumpkin seeds together, allow to cool, and grind in blender, coffee grinder, or mortar and pestle. Place herbs and carrot tops in a food processor and pulse until herbs are roughly chopped. Add the garlic, olive oil, and lemon juice and pulse/process until a chunky paste begins to come together. Add ground spices, pumpkin seeds, ground cardamom, crushed red pepper flakes, salt, and pepper. Pulse until sauce comes together and is uniform in size. Be careful not to process too much as the sauce should not resemble a uniform paste. This recipe will make 20 ounces of sauce. Heat a cast iron skillet over medium high heat. Once hot, add enough oil to coat the bottom of the skillet, season salmon with salt and place flesh side down (not the side that would have had the skin on it). Cook to desired temperature, turning once and finishing in a 425 degree oven if you prefer the fish to be on the more cooked side.

Assembly

Serve salmon with blanched broccolini (or asparagus come spring or summer time). To plate, spread 2 ounces of hummus on a plate, followed by the chosen vegetable, then the seared salmon. Top the piece of fish with a hefty spoonful of zhoug and garnish with pomegranate seeds and lemon oil. Feel free to substitute olive oil if lemon oil is not readily available.

Makes 5 cups of hummus.

▶ Tres Leches Shortcake with Caramel-Rum Sauce (cont'd)

Tres Leches Shortcake con't from page 155 evaporated milk, cinnamon stick, and clove in a sauce pan and bring to a simmer. Once simmering, continue to heat for an additional 3 minutes. After three minutes, remove from heat, cover pot, and steep for 10 minutes.

In a separate mixing bowl, combine sweetened condensed milk, vanilla, and ground cinnamon, mixing until well combined. Strain steeped milk into sweetened condensed milk mixture and stir until well combined. Allow to cool to room temperature.

Cake Assembly
Using a wooden skewer or fork, poke many holes in the cooled shortcake. Pour the milk/sweetened condensed milk liquid over cake and allow to soak up the liquid.

Caramel-Rum Sauce
To make the caramel-rum sauce, place can of sweetened condensed milk in a sauce pot and cover completely with water. Bring to a boil and continue to boil for 2 to 3 hours, adding water to ensure the can is always fully submerged in water. Remove from heat and allow to cool. Once the sweetened condensed milk is cool, place in a mixing bowl and combine with cream and rum.

Sweetened Whipped Cream
Using a stand mixer or a hand held mixer, with the whisk attachment, place cold heavy whipping cream and vanilla in a chilled mixing bowl. Whip on medium-low until soft peaks have formed. Once soft peaks have formed, add the powdered sugar and continue to whip on medium-low until stiff peaks form.

To Serve
Cover the top of the tres leches cake with sweetened whipped cream. Slice cake into desired size, move to plate, and pour at least one ounce of caramel-rum sauce over each slice.

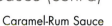

Restaurant Address and Contact Information

AV **BLUE PLATE** — 1
48 East Beaver Creek Blvd. Avon, CO
(970) 845-2252

WV **GESSNER AT HOTEL TALISIA** — 13
1300 Westhaven Dr, Vail, CO 81657
(970) 476-7111

ED **HARVEST** — 25
1265 Berry Creek Rd, Edwards, CO 81632
(970) 477-5353

ED **JUNIPER** — 37
97 Main St, Edwards, CO 81632
(970) 926-7001

VV **LA BOTTEGA** — 47
100 E Meadow Dr, Vail, CO 81657
(970) 476-0280

VV **LaNONNA** — 57
100 E Meadow Dr STE 24, Vail, CO 81657
(970) 393-5959

VV **LA TOUR** — 67
122 E Meadow Dr, Vail, CO 81657
(970) 476-4403

VV **LEFT BANK** — 79
183 Gore Creek Dr, Vail, CO 81657
(970) 476-3696

VV **LENORA AT THE SEBASTIAN** — 91
16 Vail Rd, Vail, CO 81657
(970) 477-8050

VV **LUDWIGS AT SONNENALP** — 103
20 Vail Rd, Vail, CO 81657
(970) 479-5461

BC **MIRABELLE AT BEAVER CREEK** — 115
55 Village Rd, Beaver Creek, CO 81620
(970) 949-7728

BC **SPLENDIDO AT THE CHATEAU** — 127
17 Chateau Ln, Beaver Creek, CO 81620
(970) 845-8808

VV **SWISS CHALET** — 139
20 Vail Rd, Vail, CO 81657
(970) 479-5462

VV **TERRA BISTRO AT THE VAIL MT LODGE** — 149
352 E Meadow Dr, Vail, CO 81657
(435) 649-5400

AV Avon **BC** Beaver Creek **ED** Edwards **LH** Lionshead **VV** Vail Village **WV** West Vail

BASIC MEASUREMENTS

1/16 tsp	dash		
1/8 tsp	pinch		
1 tsp		1/3 Tbsp	5 ml
1 Tbsp	1/2 oz	3 tsps	15 ml
1 cup	8 oz	16 Tbsp	240 ml
1 pint	16 oz	2 cups	473 ml
1 qt	32 oz	2 pints	946 ml
1 gal	128 oz	4 qts	3785 ml

LIQUID OR VOLUME

2 Tbsp	1 oz	1/8 cup, 6 tsps	30 ml
1/4 cup	2 oz	4 Tbsps	59 ml
1/3 cup	2 2/3 oz	5 Tbsps + 1 tsp	79 ml
1/2 cup	4 oz	8 Tbsps	118 ml
2/3 cup	5 1/3 oz	10 Tbsps + 2 tsps	158 ml
3/4 cup	6 oz	12 Tbsps	177 ml
7/8 cup	7 oz	14 Tbsps	207 ml
1 cup	8 oz	16 Tbsps	237 ml
2 cups	16 oz	32 Tbsps	473 ml
4 cups	32 oz	1 qt	946 ml
1 pint	16 oz	32 Tbsps	473 ml
2 pints	32 oz	1 qt	946 ml
8 pints	128 oz	4 qts	3785 ml
4 qts	1 gal/128 oz	1 gal	3785 ml
1 liter	1.057 qts		1000 ml
1 gal	4 qts	128 oz	3785 ml

DRY OR WEIGHT MEASUREMENTS

1/2 oz	1 Tbsp	15 gr
1 oz	2 Tbsp	30 gr
2 oz	1/4 cup	55 gr
3 oz	1/3 cup	85 gr
4 oz	1/4 lb	115 gr
8 oz	1/2 lb	226 gr
12 oz	3/4 lb	340 gr
16 oz	1 lb	454 gr
32 oz	2 lbs	907 gr
1 kg	2.2 lbs/35.2 oz	1000 gr

COOKING TEMPERATURES

Medium-rare	63°C (145°F)
Medium	71°C (160°F)
Well done	77°C (170°F)

Contributing Sommelier
CAMERON NADLER

Cameron has been in the restaurant and wine industry for over 10 years working for five star restaurants in London, Park City and New York City. Now the Beverage Manager in New York City's esteemed Ralph Lauren Polo Bar where, for over 4 years, Cameron has been curating a wine and liquor list that stretches the globe. He is thrilled to be back helping with another Park City Publishing Cookbook. This Vail edition allowed him to get to know the restaurants of Vail and pair their incredible dishes with an eclectic mix of wines of the world. Cheers to your delicious pairings!

Contributing Watercolor Artist
GARY GAUTNEY

"My paintings are inspired by an imagination developed from my early childhood travels, and the beauty of my surroundings. I take the beauty around me, add color, and my own style to make them unique and appealing. I found I had a talent with simple drawings on a scratch pad, and then I took an interest in watercolor which is where my main concentration is at the present. My work is a style of realism although you can find surrealism in many of my pieces along with hidden shapes and contrary meanings. As an artist I use color, value, energy and light as my main artistic elements when creating my compositions. My work is accomplished by working the entire composition rather than sections or objects. I paint because I love to give and share my talent. When people stop and take time to look at my work I know I have shared a part of me with them."

Contributing Photographers

PAT CONE
Over the past four decades, Patrick Cone has worked as a photographer in Los Angeles, as a helicopter photographer in Seattle, a Summit County Commissioner, a corporate photographer for Browning/Winchester, a writer and editor, and a university instructor. He has worked on assignment for publications including Arizona Highways, Skiing, Smithsonian, Sunset, National Geographic, the Wall Street Journal, Wired, and dozens of other regional and national publications. He is the author of three children's science books. Pat is currently the magazine editor at The Park Record in Park City, and the special projects editor at National Parks.
PatrickConePhotography.com

NOAH WETZEL
A freelance photographer based in Steamboat Springs Colorado and Alta, Utah, Noah Wetzel specializes in adventure, landscape, and active lifestyle imagery. Noah's love for photography and storytelling has been cultivated through his passion for the outdoors, and his work has been showcased around the world.
NoahDavidWetzel.com

SCOTT CRAMER
"I'm a people, lifestyle, commercial, architecture, travel, landscape and outdoor adventure photographer from the Vail Valley of Colorado." On most days, Scott can be found wandering around outdoors at sunrise and sunset trying to capture interesting images in the golden hour light. He is always up for an adventure and exploring new places and loves to capture other people doing what they love and who share a passion for enjoying the outdoors. Scott studied at the University of Michigan in Ann Arbor and moved to Vail over 20 years ago. He loves spending time with his family and has been known to drag them along for some of his photo adventures. Scott is passionate about photography and feels privileged doing what he loves and truly appreciates how photography is a life-long learning process.
Scottcramerphotography.com

SCOTT BELLOW
"With the silent draw of the sunny Colorado skies, and dramatic landscape, I left New Jersey to follow my dreams of adventure and to chase adrenaline. Photography has guided me towards that dream which is now my profession." Scott captures nature and life in a way that is exclusive to his vision. His goal is to create lasting memories whether its extreme sporting events, a new home, or lasting love between two people. Scott prefers to shoot authentic, real life experiences that exude raw emotion. Connected to his subjects he take pride in their lifelong meaning. When not shooting you can find Scott snowboarding, fly fishing, mountain biking, hiking, trail running, and surfing - with his camera likely attached to my hip!"
Scottbellow.com

JEFFREY HULSE
"Trust is my motto when it comes to shooting peoples one time moments. My biggest drive in my life is my Wife and two beautiful girls. I'll have to admit they are tired of me always wanting to take pictures of them, however they will appreciate it later in life. And that being said I love doing the same for others for a living!"
www.jeffreyhulse.com

Book and Jacket design and Production by: Lauren Nadler

PHOTOGRAPHY CREDITS: Cover, Snowy Bicycles, Pat Cone; Lionshead at the Arrabelle Vail Square during dusk with the gondola, Scott Cramer; Ski Racer "The Edge", Lauren Nadler; Piney Lake, Shutterstock; Johnny Lyons skiing fresh powder near Vail after a fresh snow storm, Scott Cramer; pgs 10-11, Ben Wetzel descends into the Lake Constantine valley while backpacking in the Mt. Holy Cross Wilderness, Colorado, Noah Wetzel; pg 12, Moody Piney Lake landscape, Scott Bellow; Pgs 22-23, Evening overlook of the town of Vail, Jeffrey Hulse; pg 24, Deepest day of 2018/2019 season on Vail Mountain, Scott Bellow; Pgs 34-35, Golf at Sonnenalp Club, Noah Wetzel; pg 36, Teddy "Redneck" Schweer inspecting the inside of a hot air balloon during inflation for Camelot Balloons, Scott Cramer; pg 45, Moose at Sunset Piney Lake, Scott Bellow; pg 46, Vail Clock tower, Shutterstock; pg 49, Ratatouille, Shutterstock; pg 55, Mountain meadows of Lupine and Indian Paintbrush wildflowers near Vail Pass, Scott Cramer; pg 56, Riding A10 at Sunset, Scott Bellow; pg 65, GoPro Games, Steep Creek Kayak Competition, Scott Bellow; pg 66, Summer Sunset from the Summit of Vail Mountain, Shutterstock; pg 77, Fresh Corduroy Early Morning, Scott Bellow; pg 78, Rocky Mountain Elk silhouette high above treeline, Scott Cramer; pgs 80-81, Food Images for Left Bank, Pat Cone; pgs 88-89, Aspen trees creating interesting shadows in the snow. Beaver Creek, Colorado, Scott Cramer; pg 90, Fly Fishing Ten Mile Canyon, Scott Bellow; pgs 100-101, Pack Rafting Brady Lake, Scott Bellow; pg 102, Single Track at Vail, Scott Bellow; pgs 112-113, Panorama of Mt. of the Holy Cross (left). Iconic mountain in the Sawatch Range near Vail, Colorado Rocky Mountains, Shutterstock; pg 114, Piney Lake, Vail Colorado, Shutterstock; pg 125, The Eagle Bahn Gondola, Vail Mountain, Shutterstock; pg 126, Colorado Ski Hall of Fame athlete Chris Anthony skiing fresh powder on Vail Mountain, Scott Cramer; pgs 136-137, Sunny Powder Day in Sun Down Bowl, Vail Mountain, Scott Bellow; pg 138, Aspen Grove, Vail, Colorado, Shutterstock; pg 141, Rösti, Shutterstock; pg 147, Autumn Aspen Leaves against a Colorado Sky, Shutterstock; pg 148, Kirsten Stuart Mountain biking scenic singletrack with incredible mountain views near the Gore Range, Scott Cramer; pg 159, Curious fox up high at 12,500 feet in the alpine terrain of the rugged Sawatch Mountains, Scott Cramer; pg 160, Ski Race Sculpture, Lauren Nadler; pg 163 Scenic Piney Lake. Shutterstock; pg 165, View from Gitalong Road, Scott Bellow; pg 167, Bicycles on Standby, Pat Cone; pg 168, Cowboy Ride, Pat Cone; Front and Back Covers, Snow Background, Shutterstock.

ILLUSTRATION CREDITS: Info graphic Maps of Vail, Roger Burrows. Gary Gautney: Copyright page, Measuring Spoons, pg 5, ginger, pg 9, Onions and Cilantro on Blue Plate, pg 16, Trout, pg 17, Coconut, pg 50, Tuscan Bread, pg 73, Dover Solo, pg 75, Bowl of Onions, pg 83, Dijon Mustard, pg 83, Egg and Lobster, pg. 84, Halibut, Onions and Cilantro, pg 86, Vanilla, pg 94, Hawaiian Ono, pg 106, Carton of Egg, Tomato, pg 108, Waffles, pg 122, Coconut, pg 135, Lemons, pg 142, Baguette, pg 153, Coconut, pg 154, Salmon, pg 161, Serving Utensils, pg 164, Measuring Spoons. Additional Watercolor illustrations by Shutterstock Artists.